Fundraising For Introverts

Thank you, BOTH!

Praise for *Fundraising for Introverts*

"In *Fundraising for Introverts*, Brian Saber masterfully debunks the myth of the extroverted fundraiser and makes a compelling case for the fundraising power of the introverted fundraiser—board member and staff alike. A must-read for everyone in our field!"

— *Rob Acton, Founder & CEO, Cause Strategy Partners*

"You're an introvert. And you're hired to be a fundraiser... or maybe you've just joined a board. Are you doomed... or destined for fundraising greatness? Spoiler alert: greatness... as Brian Saber's blissfully honest new book demonstrates over and over. It's a rousing pep talk and survival guide for the 51% of us who function wonderfully well as real-life introverts."

— *Tom Ahern, Author, Fundraising Marketing Guru*

"Brian Saber's new book is a terrific reminder of how much good donor relationships are based on listening, not talking."

— *Claire Axelrad, Founder and Principal, Clarification*

"Brian Saber takes his experience, compassion, and expertise and rolls it up into inspirational advice for introverted fundraisers and everyone who works with them. It you are an introvert and have any doubt in your fundraising prowess, this book will put those doubts to rest."

— *Amy Eisenstein, CEO & Founder, Capital Campaign Pro*

"We love the way Brian challenges conventional thinking that fundraisers must be loud, loquacious and silver-tongued speakers. He highlights the profound truth that introverts can be equally, if not more effective, in soliciting gifts because of their heightened listening skills and sensitivity and respect toward donor prospects."

— *Jim Eskin, Founder, Eskin Fundraising Training*

"If you're an introvert looking to make a difference in the world, Fundraising for Introverts is an absolute must-read. But it doesn't stop there—even seasoned fundraisers will find immense value in Brian's fresh perspective and insightful advice. Prepare to be inspired, emboldened, and ready to take your fundraising efforts to a whole new level."

— *Pamela Grow, Founder, Basics & More Fundraising,*
Simple Development Systems

"Brian Saber's book *Fundraising for Introverts* takes a very complicated subject and makes it seem completely understandable. Fundraising for Introverts will instantly help you understand that introverts can achieve great success just by being themselves!"

— *Andy Hamingson, Founder, Principal*
AD Hamingson & Associates

"We finally have a book that articulates the nuanced concepts and strategies an introvert can use to maximize their personality in the pursuit of fundraising for any important cause."

— *Peter Heller, Founder, Heller Fundraising Group*

"I, too, am an introvert, hiding in plain sight. I love the way Brian Saber shines a spotlight on the gifts and talents of introverted fundraisers. This book will help so many people feel more comfortable in their fundraising role. Thank you to Brian for reminding us that being authentically ourselves is always what makes us successful and happy."

— *Lori Jacobwith, Founder, Ignited Fundraising*

"Introverts rejoice! You can excel in planned giving fundraising. Brian's insights into the Asking Styles include that introverts listen attentively; question curiously; empathize; and wait patiently. Those each sit on my short list of attributes for successful Planned Giving."

—*Tony Martignetti, Planned Giving Accelerator and*
Martignetti Planned Giving Advisors, LLC

"I am an introvert and I realized more so as I read Brian's book. Being social takes a lot of energy, but like Brian I have acted as an extrovert to succeed. Am I a fake? Read the book to find out. Every fundraiser needs this book because fundraising is all about asking."

— *Viken Mikaelian, CEO, PlannedGiving.Com*

"Brian Saber's voice is smart, candid, and a breath of fresh air. Fundraising for Introverts is a calling, manifesto, and validation for a quiet revolution of introverts to claim their innate strengths and superpowers. A must-read for introverts and extroverts alike to acknowledge and celebrate the valuable traits introverts bring to fundraising."

— *Rachel Muir, CFRE, Founder Girstart, and*
League of Extraordinary Fundraisers

"Fundraising for Introverts provides a succinct and clear description of the unique qualities of introverts and aligns them brilliantly with essential aspects of the fundraising process. In so doing, it offers invaluable lessons for everyone about the dynamics of donor cultivation and stewardship. It's a must-read, especially for extroverts."

— *Marc Scorca, President/CEO, Opera America*

"If there was a Fundraising PHD Class for introverts, *Fundraising For Introverts* would be the textbook and Brian Saber would be the professor!"

— *Bob Tiede, CEO, LeadingWithQuestions.com*

"Brian Saber expertly emphasizes the fact that introverts are natural listeners and thoughtful communicators, traits that prove invaluable in the realm of individual fundraising. By guiding introverted fundraisers to embrace their unique skill set, this book instills confidence and inspires them to never apologize for who they are."

— *Greg Warner, CEO and Founder, MarketSmart*

"I am not an introvert, however I have been married to one for 48 years. I have been in fundraising for longer than I've been married. This is a must-read book for anyone asking, supervising, employed by, married to or friends with an introvert. You will never experience an introvert's behavior in the same way."

— *Carol Weisman, President, Board Builders*

"Brian Saber's new book is a must read for introverts and extroverts alike! As an extrovert, this text greatly helped me understand my colleagues and provides a deeper dive into what makes them and their skill set needed and valued. When introverts like Brian speak, it's imperative for us to listen!"

— *Lynne Wester, Founder and Principal, The DRG Group*

"I'm not an introvert, but I still found plenty of takeaway value-bombs here. Brian Saber's fundraising book is a game-changer! Get ready to make an impact while staying true to YOU! Don't miss this must-read gem!"

—*Rhea Wong, Founder, Rhea Wong Consulting*

Fundraising
For Introverts

Harnessing Our Powers for What Matters

Brian Saber

Fundraising for Introverts

Printed in the United States of America

ISBN: 978-1-961869-02-8

Book & cover design by Thomas Edward West of Amarna Books and Media
Photographs of Brian Saber by Stuart Tyson

Contents

This book is dedicated to my fellow introverts.

I see you.

Foreword

Over my 30-year career in non-profit fundraising, I have had the pleasure of working alongside amazing mentors, leaders and fundraisers. I have met and partnered with numerous fundraising consultants and experts in the field, and I can attest that Brian Saber is at the top of that field.

When I was asked by Brian to write this foreword, I was both honored and humbled that he would ask me to lend my expertise and thoughts on this topic. As CEO of two different national non-profit health organizations, the Sjogren's Foundation and now the Arthritis Foundation, I have had the pleasure of working with Brian as he consulted me and my staff (and our volunteers) about fundraising and Asking Styles. Brian has the ability to ensure that each individual, introvert or extrovert, understands and is able to capitalize on their strengths.

As an extroverted fundraiser myself, hearing Brian speak on the topic of introverts and then reading his new book, I am once again sold on how instrumental introverts are to fundraising. Each of us, introverts and extroverts, approaches fundraising differently, but both with the same intent, hope and desire to make a difference for our mission, cause or charity. My approach as an outgoing extrovert isn't the only style that works. Quiet, focused introverts can be just as effective in closing lucrative major gifts, sponsorships, and building strong donor relationships.

Throughout the following pages, you will quickly realize, as I did, how adept Brian is at identifying personality strengths, helping each person believe in themselves and convincing us all that anyone can be an effective fundraiser. Brian will share insight into the different approaches introverts and extroverts utilize in fundraising as he humbly shares personal stories as well as stories of others that enlighten us about how introverts make great fundraisers.

Brian reminds us that introverts often carry the heart of an organization, deep in their soul. They sometimes understand the mission better than us extroverts. They listen fully to those they meet with and only talk when it can be impactful. And when understood and valued, as well as when they believe in themselves, introverts can turn that heart into powerful fundraising success.

Recently, a number of Arthritis Foundation staff participated in a fundraising training led by Brian. After the training, I heard from many but most powerful was those that were introverts, who shared with me how impactful Brian was. One of them said to me, "It is the first time I wasn't ashamed of being an introvert in fundraising." Another said, "This gave me the freedom to understand I can do it my way and still be successful." And one extroverted supervisor told me, "I am so happy to better understand how introverts work and how they, too, can be very successful fundraisers."

So as an introvert, extrovert, or supervisor of an introverted fundraiser, I guarantee that you will learn from Brian's wisdom and years of experience. As a successful introverted fundraiser himself, Brian surely knows how to walk the talk!

—*Steven Taylor, President and CEO*
The Arthritis Foundation

Introduction

I am a fundraiser. I am also an introvert. For me, this book is truly a labor of love.

I've been presenting and training on the art and science of fundraising for 14 years now, and the most rewarding feedback I've gotten has come from my fellow introverts. Countless times I've heard:

"This is the first time I felt anyone has talked to me as an introvert and fundraiser."

"I never thought I could be a good fundraiser until I heard you speak."

"You have given me the confidence I never had."

This feedback has come from staff and board members alike, telling me more needed to be written on the subject. In fact, I had been noodling with a book about fundraising and introverts for years, and had even written some chapters here and there, but I put it aside twice to publish books on boards and board members.

Then two things happened.

First was COVID. For me, and for a lot of introverts, the last few years have been much easier socially than for extroverts. Though we all missed being with people, introverts were able to cope better given how we're wired. Given that we already needed a good deal of alone/down time to recharge. Given that the quiet has been our friend.

Early in the pandemic my friends called me The COVID Poster Child.

All my work travel had halted, much of my work had been

cancelled, and I had more alone time than ever as I lived alone. Though I definitely felt alone and isolated at times, I still had the good luck and resources others didn't, and the ability to remain very protected against COVID.

With that perspective, I decided to see the cup as half full and used the time to get in great shape, write a book, and complete a large jigsaw puzzle every two to three days...without looking at the picture as I went along! In the silence and solitude, I found a path forward. I believe the decreased social activity gave me the gift of focus and energy I find hard to harness otherwise. I love deep relationships with people, but the interactions can still deplete me, and having so much of that quiet and alone time gave me a certain peace.

Second, last spring, following a training in Kansas City for the Arthritis Foundation, two attendees told the CEO, Steve Taylor, that my session had been "life-changing." Through Steve, I heard that it was the first time they felt anyone had talked to them given their personalities. The first time they had been heard. That proved to be the impetus I needed to sit down and put pen to paper.

It was time to help my fellow introverted fundraisers to have complete confidence in their amazing skillset. I wanted them to be understood and appreciated for everything they bring to the table. I wanted them to know it was totally fine not to be the life of the party, the one who easily schmoozed everyone in a room, the one who effortlessly picked up the phone to chat with people they didn't know. And I wanted extroverts to appreciate us fully.

But why another book on introverts? The topic of introverts has been much discussed lately and there are several books in the field today about the introvert/extrovert dichotomy. Susan

Cain's *Quiet: The Power of Introverts in a World That Can't Stop Talking* is one of the best known and was life-changing for me.

My goal was specific, though: I felt the issue was significant enough in the fundraising field to warrant its own book, especially as there are so many introverts in the field...as there are in life.

Yes, there are lots of us, contrary to what is often assumed due to the stereotype of a fundraiser and the stereotype of an introvert. That might surprise you given the bias against introverts and the misconception many hold that introverts are a small minority. Yet according to a large-scale Myers-Briggs study, introverts actually make up slightly more than half—50.7%—of the general population, with extroverts making up 49.3%. And almost 56% of those who have taken my company's Asking Styles quiz (Chapter 4) are introverts. Other studies show similar patterns, and the idea that there are far fewer introverts has been proven to be nothing more than a bias.

While beyond the Asking Styles results there isn't much data in our field on how many fundraisers are introverts, we can safely assume we are well represented for a variety of reasons.

First, most people come to the nonprofit world due to their inner passion and their desire to make an impact in people's lives. Very few people say, "I want to be a fundraiser when I grow up!" They come to it as adults because they love the arts but aren't artists, or they care deeply about education but aren't teachers, or they want to save our planet and aren't scientists.

While introverts might at first think fundraising isn't a field for them because of the stereotype of a fundraiser, they push through those hesitations to make an impact in the world.

Executive directors, many of whom have risen from program positions, find themselves fundraising...and we can safely assume many of them are introverts. They lead organizations because of their vision, program acumen, and leadership skills, not their extroversion.

Added to this, we have millions of board members, all being asked to fundraise. While the construct of a board and its group dynamics might entice more extroverts than introverts, for certain there are tons of introverted board members who have joined for the same reasons many of us become fundraisers—to be of service.

Together, given the millions of introverts in fundraising, a book helping everyone understand introverted fundraisers felt important.

And it seemed like I was the one to write it for two reasons.

First, I'm an introverted fundraiser and I could speak both from the heart and from a lifetime of experience navigating the world as both an introvert and a fundraiser. I could talk about how I've acted since I was young, how I've managed to participate socially even when it was challenging, how I've often come across as an extrovert, and how all this has impacted how I acted as a fundraiser and how I dealt with the parts of the job that challenged me given my personality.

Second, I had developed the Asking Styles with my former business partner Andrea Kihlstedt. The Styles, which you'll learn more about later, are based on two personality traits, the first of which is how you interact—are you extroverted or introverted? For the past 14 years I've been living and breathing the Asking Styles, seeing the world through that lens. I've led more than 500 webinars on the topic, written two books expressly about them, trained more than 100 organizations using the Styles, and developed other training products and services with the Styles at their core. All to say I've been studying this topic both actively and passively for a long time.

Though my number one hope is for this book to empower introverted fundraisers to feel completely validated and totally comfortable in their roles, I also hope extroverts will read this book and come to understand and appreciate us for everything we offer the field. Spoiler alert—we introverts are great fundraisers who bring uniquely strong critical skills to the table. We are overlooked or undervalued at great peril!

—*Brian Saber*

Chapter One

Who Am I?

Many, even in my closer circles, don't believe I'm an introvert. There are lots of reasons, but the top two are their misunderstanding of me, and their misunderstanding of what an introvert is. Being a board member is a noble effort. It can be incredibly rewarding, but also quite challenging. So much is asked of you in return for the wonderful feeling that you're making a difference in the world.

People see me out on the speaking and training circuit, confidently sharing my ideas and being Mr. Articulate. They see me engaging my webinar audiences enthusiastically. They see me giving my family and friends an online singing concert during COVID. They see my great social skills. And they think I'm an extrovert.

Even my mother thought I was an extrovert. Here's what she wrote a few years back when I asked for her thoughts on my introversion and shyness.

> Amazing Brian–Shy No More!
>
> Yes, I am the proud mother of a much-wanted child. Brian was a delight: a happy and friendly child with his family. But when the doorbell rang or we met people in the village, he froze. He would hide behind his dad or me and not come out to say hello or smile. We thought middle-child syndrome! We were wrong. Brian developed into a very verbal child and person—and a caring one—out to make this a better world.
>
> Proud Mom,
>
> Elaine Saber

My own mom assumed the introverted (and shy!) kid had grown out of it. She saw how I acted as opposed to how I felt, she conflated introverted and shy, and she too thought an introvert was someone who only wanted to hang out with a book or puzzle. In fact, I am still that kid—comfortable with my family and close friends (on an individual basis and in moderation!), but ready to hide behind someone rather than meet someone new or socialize in a group.

We'll talk a good deal about these stereotypes. But to start, who from the entertainment world do you think is an introvert? You'd be surprised to know who my fellow introverts are. Not to compare myself with these legends, but did you know Oprah Winfrey and Jerry Seinfeld are introverts?! You might not see Oprah that way initially as she's such a public figure and literally made her name interacting with people throughout the quarter-century run of The Oprah Winfrey Show. But think about it for a moment.

Who's actually doing the talking? Not Oprah. In fact, most of what she's doing is listening. She's asking great questions and listening, making her guests the center of attention. As for Jerry Seinfeld, he's in good company as many actors are shy and/or introverted but feel more comfortable onstage, in a role and perhaps a costume, and at a distance from the audience.

To really introduce myself here, sometimes there's nothing like a good personal example, and reflecting on some of my own stories has helped me understand myself and the world so much better. So, although this isn't a memoir, I will share some personal stories with you. My fellow introverts will understand completely. Those who were present at these moments will be surprised. Some of you will have a well-earned chuckle. Here's the first.

Personal Story I: Hudson Guild

Picture this: It's the fall of 2007. I'm the executive director at Hudson Guild, a nonprofit serving New York City's Chelsea neighborhood. I rose to that position after six very successful years as deputy executive director (the chief fundraiser).

This particular night is the Guild's annual community dinner. It's not a fundraiser, but a friend-raiser. It's being held in the decidedly downscale main hall of our painfully institutional 1960's-era senior center. The lights are intentionally set low so the cinderblock walls, linoleum flooring, and overall shabby nature of the place won't be so obvious. Fancy this is not.

A great mix of people fills the room: lots of staff, some volunteers, participants from various programs, community leaders, Guild board members and donors, and our elected officials. I know just about everyone, and am confident that I'm well-regarded and respected, and that people are very pleased with my leadership to date. Some are even here specifically to hear my remarks over dinner.

That sounds great, right? Well, guess where I am? In the hallway, on the other side of the swinging double doors. I tell my staff I'd rather be anywhere in the world—the Gulag, perhaps—than have to walk into that room to mingle some more and, on top of that, make a speech. I've already overdosed on uncomfortable, anxiety-inducing social interactions during the reception and want nothing more than to go home. Semi-jokingly, I offer my staff a $1,000 contribution to the Guild if I don't have to go in. They respectfully decline.

With no good option, I go into Super Social Mode and dive in. I bop from table to table, meeting some people for the first time (very hard!), engaging everyone, creating tons of good will, making deeper connections. When it's time for my remarks, I knock them out of the park.

At the end of the evening, after everyone has left, I want nothing more than to be by myself. I don't care to go out and celebrate our successful event. I don't want to debrief with anyone. I crave solitude...and perhaps a crossword puzzle.

For the hundredth time, I wonder to myself how I got here. How did I end up in a position significantly focused on building relationships? How can someone who hates large groups, cringes at the thought of having to introduce himself to someone he doesn't know, and avoids the telephone, be meant for this work?

Surely there are lots of people who would be better at my role. People who like events. People who aren't shy and enjoy meeting new people. People who easily pick up the phone to chat with donors.

Am I a fake? A sham? Has my career been misguided? Are there people who have it all?

Fifteen years later, and more than a decade after founding Asking Matters and developing the Asking Styles, I'm proud to say a resounding NO! I'm not a fake or a sham. I was meant to be a fundraiser. I was meant to help organizations help people. This was my calling, and I've done a great job.

No one has it all. I have a great set of skills. We all do.

Chapter Two

Introverted, Shy, or Both

First, we must define some terms. People toss the words "introvert" and "extrovert" around with only the vaguest notion of what they truly mean. And they often conflate introversion and shyness, which we'll unpack as well.

But even before diving into these terms, I want to touch on a third term—"ambivert"—as there is much talk about this classification these days. Some say it is someone who has a complete balance of introverted and extroverted qualities. Some say it's a person who has some indicators of both traits.

Very few people are exactly 50% on either side of any dichotomy. We all tend to be more or less of one thing or another. Most of those we say are ambidextrous in reality favor one hand or the other, with only 1% of the population being truly ambidextrous.

When it comes to sexuality, though the data is less clear because of privacy issues, a recent Gallup poll found that 4% of the United States population is bisexual. However, again, that does not mean that 4% of the population has no preference, ever, in terms of who attracts them. Sexuality exists on a spectrum.[1]

I believe that virtually no one is equally introverted and extroverted. We're all on a spectrum here, as we are with dexterity and sexuality. Some of you reading about introverts will say the description fits you to a tee. Others will say you feel that way sometimes, or in some respects.

My goal here is not to pigeonhole anyone, but rather to raise awareness of how those who are more introverted than not make their way in the world and contribute to the field of fundraising.

What's an Introvert, Exactly?

People don't fully comprehend the precise meaning of introversion, although Susan Cain's inspiring best-selling book, Quiet, has done much to dispel misconceptions and give those of us who are introverted our due.

Most people hear the word "introvert" and think "anti-social," that introverts don't like being with people. It's not true that introverts aren't social; it's just that, as I well know, being

---

[1] Jones, Jeffrey M. "LGBT Identification in U.S. Ticks Up to 7.1%." Gallup, February 17, 2022. https://news.gallup.com/poll/389792/lgbt-identification-ticks-up.aspx. Accessed May 23, 2023.

social takes a lot of energy.

The terms introvert and "extravert" were developed by Carl Jung in 1921. Jung saw the introvert as someone with "an inward flowing of personal energy—a withdrawal concentrating on subjective factors. The introvert is usually happy alone with a rich imagination and prefers reflection to activity."[2]

Introverts derive energy from being by themselves and expend energy when they are with others. Extroverts are just the opposite: They derive energy from being with others (or at least are better at managing the use of energy—see below). When a party ends, the extroverts have been fueled and are ready for the next party. Introverts need to head home to recharge.

This has never been clearer to me than when I speak at conferences (I never attend them as a participant!). Here's what unfolds every time: At the end of the day the extroverts say, "Let's head to the hotel bar—who's coming?" while the introverts try to look invisible in an attempt to head to their rooms or off to a one-on-one dinner with a peer. Amusingly, I throw down the gauntlet during my trainings by using this as an example, which only encourages the extroverts to try to get me to the bar. They're 0–50, or thereabouts; I have never joined them.

Think to Talk or Talk to Think

In the broadest terms, introverts think to talk, and extroverts talk to think. Extroverts think on their feet, quickly and concisely, and this enables them to comfortably share their ideas at a fast pace—seemingly as the ideas come to them. Introverts think more deeply and expansively, and therefore need to think first and

---

[2] Jung, Carl Gustav, "Psychological Types", 1921.

then talk when those same ideas feel complete enough to share. This causes introverts to pause more often and for longer stretches before talking. And this all emanates from how we're wired.

Research has shown that extroverts and introverts use different primary brain pathways when thinking. An introvert's pathway is longer, more complex, and internally focused while the extrovert's is shorter, more straightforward, and externally focused.

Introverts also draw more on long-term memory, versus extroverts who draw on short-term memory. Hence the reason why introverts need longer to respond... and why we can get tongue-tied when we talk or respond too quickly. Personally, I notice I often repeat what I've said, and I believe it's because I blurted it out quickly the first time before my brain could fully synthesize my response.

The time an introvert needs to think before speaking can create a challenge depending on the rhythm of a conversation. Certainly, our preferred slower rhythm is not the usual rhythm at a party or in many group settings, where the conversation ricochets quickly and the person who thinks of what to say fastest gets to talk more. Therefore, to be in the mix in a group setting, introverts unconsciously try to speed up—or end up shortchanging—their processing time to talk before someone else chimes in. This speeding up of the process uses even more energy, depleting introverts even more.

Though this fast dynamic can still exist in one-on-one settings, here an introvert does have more control over the pace of the conversation. Assuming the other party is aware of themselves and has sensitivity to the introvert, they will have no choice but to slow down and wait for a response before chiming in again.

There's a second energy dynamic at work here based on how we respond to external stimulation. Neurotransmitters are chemical messengers that are key to how we act. Two key neurotransmitters are dopamine and acetylcholine. Dopamine is the chemical in the brain that, when released, motivates us to seek external rewards. Acetylcholine is the feel-good chemical in our brain, and it is released when we turn inward to focus on things that matter to us and, importantly here, when we have meaningful conversation.

Dopamine is found to be more active in extroverts, whereas acetylcholine is found to be more active in introverts. So, extroverts are wired to expend energy as they see every interaction as a possible reward. Introverts are wired to conserve energy and see those same outward interactions as potential liabilities.

Jenn Granneman, a thought leader on introversion, puts the concept of rewards this way:

> "For adults, rewards are things like money, social status, social affiliation, and even sex and food...Of course, introverts care about things like money, relationships, and food, too. However, researchers believe that introverts are wired to respond differently to rewards than extroverts do. Compared to the more outgoing among us, we "quiet ones" are simply less motivated and energized by these same rewards. It's like extroverts see big, juicy steaks everywhere, while introverts mostly see overcooked hamburgers."[3]

---

3 Granneman, Jenn. "Why Do Introverts Love Being Alone? Here's the Science." Introvert, Dear, January 12, 2023, https://introvertdear.com/news/introverts-alone-time-science-marti-olsen-laney/. Accessed May 23, 2023.

Of course, this impacts the motivation for fundraising. Extroverts are generally more motivated to hit big goals and make big impacts; they get bigger rewards from this due to their dopamine levels. Introverts are motivated to build deep relationships and have meaningful conversations with donors, conversations that bring donors closer to the organization.

Are all introverts shy?
Or all shy people introverts?

People often incorrectly conflate introversion and shyness.

Whereas introversion is based on the energy it takes to think and interact, shyness is based on the fear of how one will be judged when one interacts. The opposite of shyness isn't extroversion, it's being outgoing—being the person who isn't afraid to approach strangers in a meeting or at a party, who isn't concerned with how their thoughts will be judged.

This does not mean some people aren't both shy and introverted, and being born with more-reactive temperaments can create a predisposition for people to be both.

So, why do people conflate them, and what's the difference? Primarily, people miss the difference because the outcomes for both can be the same. The shy and the introverted both veer away from various social situations. Both are apt to turn down party invitations, say little in group settings, and display what can look like a hesitance to speak up.

However, their motivations are different. Shy people will avoid social situations because they fear feeling bad about themselves in these situations. They may fear not being included in conversations, saying the wrong thing and facing ridicule, or missing social cues and misspeaking. Introverts veer away from these situations because they know how draining they will be, and because these situations don't bring them the same pleasures they bring extroverts.

Interestingly, with all the negative messages introverts get, they can become shyer over time as they avoid situations where they'll be judged. For instance, how often has someone commented on my standing by a wall at a party? (Story to follow.) Here I've made the effort to come, and I'm being told that's not good enough. That I should mingle more. That makes me even more reticent when the next party comes along.

Similarly, a shy person may seem to become more introverted over time. Since socializing can be challenging, a shy person learns to seek out smaller and more controlled social circumstances, if they seek out those circumstances at all. The shy person is more likely to figure out how to be even more fulfilled spending time alone.

By the way, the same mislabeling can be true for the outgoing and the extroverts. Both willingly engage lots of people, though extroverts do it based on a need to derive energy from others, while outgoing folks have a deep desire to meet new people. Further, extroverts can be shy—feeling the need to be around others but fearing rejection in that pursuit.

Given how people perceive shyness, incorrectly confusing shyness and introversion can further devalue the great strengths of introverts. Shyness has long been thought of as a liability at best—or, at worst, as a personality disorder.

Susan Cain, in an op-ed for *The New York Times*, highlighted recent research which sheds important light on introversion and shyness. She noted that "shyness and introversion share an undervalued status in a world that prizes extroversion...As a society, we prefer action to contemplation, risk-taking to heed-taking, certainty to doubt. Studies show that we rank fast and frequent talkers as more competent, likable and even smarter than slow ones."[4]

Writing in *Psychology Today*, Dr. Barbara Markway, a clinical psychologist and author of two books on shyness, states: "I sometimes feel that shy people are labeled in a way that places them at the bottom of any social desirability hierarchy. What's so wrong with being shy anyway?"[5]

In fact, shy and/or introverted people have been important leaders in our world. I did some research here and found Mahatma Gandhi, Abraham Lincoln, and Bill Gates among the lists of venerable shy leaders. So are Dr. Seuss, Michael Jordan, and Rosa Parks.

Cain also made a case in that op-ed that I really appreciated. She posited that if, in fact, shyness and introversion were such detriments, wouldn't the shy and introverted be extinct by now? Since they're not, we can safely assume the shy and introverted of the world must have developed some great survival techniques!

Cain noted:

> "We even find 'introverts' in the animal kingdom, where
> 15 percent to 20 percent of many species are watchful,
> slow-to-warm-up types who stick to the sidelines (some-

4 Cain, Susan. "Shyness: Evolutionary Tactic?" *The New York Times*, June 25, 2011.

5 Markway, Barbara, "A Quiet Rant About Introversion and Shyness", *Psychology Today*, February 12, 2013.

times called 'sitters') while the other 80 percent are 'rovers' who sally forth without paying much attention to their surroundings. Sitters and rovers favor different survival strategies, which could be summed up as the sitter's 'Look before you leap' versus the rover's inclination to 'Just do it!' Each strategy reaps different rewards."

Those with sitter-like temperaments tend to learn by observing instead of by acting. Sitters digest information thoroughly, stay on task, and—as Cain points out—have "a willingness to listen to and implement other people's ideas."

And that is where introverts and fundraising intersect perfectly.

Chapter Three

Introverts Are
Great Fundraisers

Obviously, I think we introverts can be great fundraisers...otherwise I wouldn't have written this book. I just wish it hadn't taken me 25 years to figure that out through my work developing the Asking Styles. In fact, all those years I thought I was an imposter of sorts. My bosses and organizations were very happy with my work, but I couldn't help but think there must be someone who could do what I was doing AND enjoy special events, excel at networking and meeting people, enjoy chatting on the phone, etc.

I wish I had figured it out 25 years ago not only for me, but so that I could put my fellow introverted fundraisers on a pedestal way back when—and so I could tell everyone else in our industry that they ignored or devalued us at their peril. That we are integral to fundraising and embracing us will always strengthen their team.

Let's talk about the ways in which introverts excel.

Listening, Not Talking— The Ultimate Superpower

As the late, great fundraising guru Jerry Panas once said, "No one ever listened themselves out of a gift." Classic Jerry, and so true.

Fundraising is about building relationships, and building relationships is based on how people communicate with, and come to trust, each other. When we're trying to build a relationship between two individuals, the key to building the relationship is the ability to listen to one another. In fact, listening is often cited as the most important trait in fundraising, especially in individual gift work. It's also true in our efforts to build relationships with foundation staff, corporate giving officers, and our elected officials and their staffs.

Well, this is great news for us introverts as, hands down, our number one superpower is that we're good listeners. Yes, we have a significant advantage in what is often considered the most important trait in fundraising. Think about that for a second: While the stereotype says introverts are at a disadvantage as fundraisers, in fact we have a distinct advantage in the art of building relationships with donors. So, why is listening so important—and why do introverts do it so much better?

In a conversation, one is either talking or listening. The rule of thumb in fundraising is to talk less than 50% of the time. The goal is to get the donor to do most of the talking, as much as 65% or 75%.

If we were to do all the talking, we'd create what's called a wall of words, where we've talked so much one of two things happens. Either the donor stops listening to us because our voice has become white noise, or the donor listens intermittently and may very well not hear—or remember—the most important points we're making.

It's often said that humans remember the least of what they hear. They remember more of what they say, even more of what they do, and the most about how they feel. If we as fundraisers do all the talking, we risk our donors feeling talked at. We risk their feeling we're selling them. We risk them not feeling good when the meeting is over. And we risk them not taking away from the conversation what was most important to take away.

However, if we engage them with questions and demonstrate that we are interested in learning about them, they'll feel important...which they are. They'll walk away feeling great about the meeting. They'll remember the important stuff. And we'll have learned much more about them, which will enable us to customize our cultivation, solicitation, and stewardship.

Because we introverts are wired to talk less and listen more, it's easier for us to give our donors greater opportunity to ask questions, share their viewpoints, and talk themselves into a gift.

Extroverts can struggle on this front. Though their ease at chatting can be helpful in opening conversations and keeping them moving along, extroverts have a tendency to talk too much. The brief silences in a meeting can drive them nuts and they will rush to fill them, whereas the introverts can sit with that silence. The silence gives our donors an opportunity to say something more.

In fact, our donors often need that time to say something more. Research shows it can take eight to ten seconds to formulate a good answer to a question that requires thought. Take a moment and count to eight. It's a long time, right?

People often take less time to answer a question than they really need because they are trying to accommodate the questioner and the long silence can be challenging for both parties. Even four or five seconds of silence will sound like a lot.

Further, questioners often speak again too quickly. How long do we generally wait before adding something to our question or rephrasing the question? Research shows it's as little as two or three seconds. That does not bode well for having a meaningful, intentional conversation.

Now imagine if a particular donor is an introvert. Though we'll talk more about donors later, it's important to note that we can assume, all things being equal, that half our donors are introverts, just as half the population is. Half our donors are likely to pause more than less before speaking. If we rush to fill the space and cut them off, we are likely to create some friction or negativity, not to mention lose the opportunity to learn something new.

While most fundraisers could probably benefit from slowing down a conversation with a donor, introverted fundraisers naturally give a conversation more room to breathe. They understand, personally, the need to take time to formulate an answer, and are more likely to provide that space to others. That's an incredible asset.

Being Caring and Empathetic

If listening is an introvert's top superpower, being caring, attentive, and empathetic is close behind, especially for Kindred Spirits—one of the two types of introverts in the Asking Styles framework. Kindred Spirits are wired to want to help. They strive to find out what makes someone tick and what they need, and then meet that need. Often, they meet the need with words of acknowledgment and concern. They are most likely to use an emotional connection to communicate to donors that they hear them and care.

Mission Controllers—the other group of introverts we'll learn about in the next chapter—show they care by listening and helping to find a solution. What's the plan? What can be done to address this situation? How can I make sure your needs are met? They excel at finding solutions to a donor's needs.

Responding to a donor in a caring and empathic way deepens the relationship as it would any personal or business relationship. It proves we're listening and that we're attuned to our donors' needs and desires. It underscores they're important to us and, by extension, our organizations. And, in this day and age when the disconnect in society often feels so great, that makes an even greater impact on our donors.

Bonding Through the Personal

A third key strength when building relationships is the ability to share personal stories, experiences and perspectives that validate each other. In many ways this is the next logical step to listening and showing empathy. First, we listen. Then we show that we empathize with what we have heard. And, in an ideal situation, we also share something personal that demonstrates we understand what the other is communicating.

One can see where extroverts might struggle, for without giving someone the opportunity to speak, and then taking the time to truly listen, any attempt at empathy could sound insincere. Introverts, and Kindred Spirits in particular, shine brightly here.

Imagine the impact of this in fundraising. Imagine sitting in a cultivation meeting, asking a donor what they think of your organization, and hearing they have some concerns. You're probably surprised, and a bit thrown. What to do? What's most important here is to continue listening, to say you hear what the donor is saying, and to ask further questions to better understand what the issue is. It's important to contain that first impulse to counter their argument, try to change their mind by providing data, or reinforce your own enthusiasm for the project.

Now imagine you're in a meeting where you've just asked for a gift and the response is awkward. Perhaps the donor has shared some very personal financial information which makes the requested gift more than a stretch. What do you say? This is another moment when listening, empathizing, and making your donor feel comfortable are paramount. If you seem mercenary and immediately come up with solutions without asking questions, you risk devaluing the donor's relationship to the organization. The long view is what's important, which plays to the strength of Mission Controllers (planning) and Kindred Spirits (caring).

Given all this, you might assume introverts are better fundraisers. Well, we don't have data on that, and I will refrain from coming to a biased conclusion! However, studies have been conducted in the for-profit sales arena, and the results were quite the opposite of what most expected. In fact, in one significant study of more than 4,000 salespeople, there was virtually no correlation between extroversion and sales performance (0.07%).[6]

---

[6] Barrick, Murray R., et al. "Personality and Performance at the Beginning of the New Millennium: What Do We Know and Where Do We Go Next?" International Journal of Selection and Assessment, Vol. 9, March/June 2001, pp. 9–30.

So, fellow introverts, wear your skills loud and proud. They are serving you incredibly well in your donor relationships. You are creating space for your donors. You are building bridges to them. You are allowing them to be front and center, and to be heard. And you're learning a ton.

VOICES FROM THE FIELD

ESTHER LANDAU (*Mission Contoller/Kindred Spirit*)
Senior Director, Advancement
The Arc San Francisco

When I started working in fundraising, I hadn't even really figured out that I was an introvert. I knew I felt awkward and clumsy in conversation with new people, especially when I needed to seem smooth and confident. I kept looking for ways to make myself change—to pretend to be the outgoing, dynamic person I thought I had to be. But the longer I stuck with the work, the more I found that being bad at small talk meant I'm really good at deep talk. And deep talk builds authentic connection. I didn't have to pretend to be an extrovert to get by. I needed to lean into my introversion.

Chapter Four

Asking Styles

Now let's put this in the context of the Asking Styles.

While we can fantasize about the ideal fundraiser who has it all, doesn't it make more sense for each of us to embrace our own personality and fundraise in a way that will work for us? Of course there are best practices, but to the extent that fundraising—in particular, the individual cultivation and solicitation of donors—is about building relationships, authenticity is key. And that means bringing one's unique personality to the table.

Andrea Kihlstedt and I met at Hudson Guild, where she served as our capital campaign consultant. We became fast friends, and after I left the Guild we started to think about how we could help people embrace who they are and fundraise more comfortably and effectively. Together we came to develop a system to help fundraisers discover their personality type, apply their unique strengths, and work at their particular challenges. We named the system Asking Styles.

We based the Asking Styles on two personality traits we thought were key to how we fundraise.

The first trait is how we interact with people. Are we extroverted or introverted? This is based on where we derive our energy, as we examined earlier. To recap, extroverts derive their energy from being with others, and introverts derive their energy from themselves and expend it with others. Much of this has to do with whether we are more sensitive to dopamine (extroverted) or acetylcholine (introverted).

how do you interact with people?

extrovert	=	derive energy from others	talk to think
introvert	=	derive energy from oneself	think to talk

The second characteristic is how we take in and synthesize information. Are we analytic or intuitive? Analytics look at the facts and then come up with an idea based on them. Intuitives start with a gut idea and then see if the facts support it. Whether we start with facts or a gut idea impacts why we love our organization in the first place, what we find most important about it, and how we will present it when talking to others. And for introverts, whether we're analytics or intuitives, our longer neural pathways will cause us to take longer to synthesize information and present our ideas.

how do you take in information?

$$\text{analytic} = \frac{\substack{\text{inductive} \\ \text{fact-oriented}}}{\text{data to idea}} \quad \Big| \quad \text{intuitive} = \frac{\substack{\text{deductive} \\ \text{idea-oriented}}}{\text{idea to data}}$$

When we put the two axes together, we get the four Asking Styles:

Rainmaker: Analytic Extrovert
Go-Getter: Intuitive Extrovert
Kindred Spirit: Intuitive Introvert
Mission Controller: Analytic Introvert

Here's a brief description of the four Asking Styles. As you read through them, see if one sounds more like you (or someone you know) than the others. Later in this chapter, we'll share a link to a quiz through which you can learn your own Asking Style.

At Asking Matters we always start top left and go clockwise, so I will do that here—though that in no way should be seen as a pecking order with introverts at the end!

Rainmakers

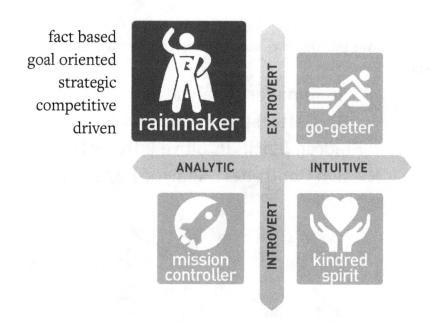

fact based
goal oriented
strategic
competitive
driven

We start with Rainmakers, the analytic extroverts. Rainmakers are very objective; they're fact-based, goal-oriented, strategic, competitive, and driven. The information they gather and analyze informs their decisions.

Rainmakers are energized by interactions with others and view developing relationships as a strategic and important process.

Driven and competitive, they enjoy the prospect of succeeding in a field so full of resistance.

However, Rainmakers in their drive to succeed, and to succeed quickly, can shortchange the process. They struggle to have the kind of deep, exploratory conversations that engage donors and reveal so much.

Go-Getters

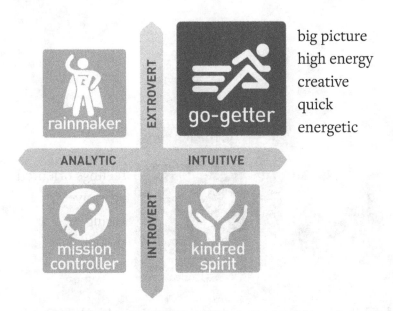

Go-Getters are intuitive extroverts who act on instinct and connect to donors through their energy and friendliness. They're big-picture, high-energy, creative, quick, and engaging types. They have a love of people and make friends easily. They are often the people you notice when they walk into a room.

Go-Getters base decisions on intuition rather than on analysis. This results in the ability to think quickly and fluidly, which enables them to relate well to donors. Go-Getters are extroverts with a natural enthusiasm and energy that draws people to them.

Where Go-Getters struggle is in their efforts to tamp down their enthusiasm, stop talking, and take the time to listen closely to others.

And now for our two introverted Asking Styles:

Kindred Spirits

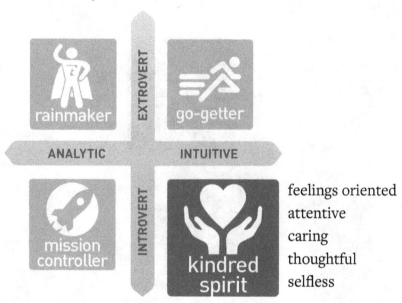

feelings oriented
attentive
caring
thoughtful
selfless

Kindred Spirits are intuitive introverts. I'm a Kindred Spirit. We Kindred Spirits bring a deep, personal passion to our cause and connect to donors through a deep commitment to the work. Kindred Spirits base decisions on intuition, and those decisions come from deep wells of emotion. We wear our hearts on our sleeves.

As discussed earlier, we draw energy from internal experiences and are more likely to enjoy one-on-one interactions. We have a strong desire to selflessly help those in need and want others to do the same. We tend to be attentive, caring, and thoughtful, which are great qualities for fundraisers as we naturally pay attention to others and their needs in the hopes of making them feel good.

One thing for Kindred Spirits to be mindful of is that although we think to talk and have a slower conversational rhythm, silence can make us nervous. In that nervousness, Kindred Spirits will sometimes start talking to fill the silence—which, as I mentioned earlier, isn't always what's needed. Often, the silences themselves bear the fruit.

Mission Controllers

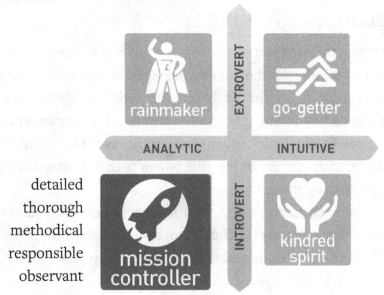

Mission Controllers are analytic introverts—quietly thoughtful and always with a wealth of information at the ready. Mission Controllers are great listeners and observers, which makes them effective solicitors. They place value on gathering and analyzing information, and approach their work systematically and methodically, making sure to dot their i's and cross their t's.

Mission Controllers are the best when it comes to sitting back and waiting for a response. First, their systematic and planful nature means they'll follow the plan... and the plan is not to talk. Second, listening is in their sweet spot since they'd rather listen and observe than talk.

The Achilles' heel for Mission Controllers is their tendency to be rigid. They've planned so carefully and fully that any deviation from their plan can throw them off. It's harder for them to go with the flow, as might need to happen when they hear something different from a donor than what they've expected.

Secondary Asking Styles

Are you thinking you're a little bit of this and a little bit of that? For most of us, even though one Asking Style stands out, we see a fair amount of another Style in us as well. Few of us fit neatly and completely in one quadrant or another. I call those who do the "uber-Rainmakers," "uber-Go-Getters," etc. The "ubers" are in the farthest corners of the grid, where both characteristics are equally, and significantly, dominant.

For most of us, one characteristic is more dominant than the other. Either our extroversion, introversion, analytic thinking, or intuitive thinking dominates. To reflect this, we also identify a Secondary Asking Style.

For instance, you can be a Mission Controller/Rainmaker, in which case your analytic trait is dominant, and you might well find yourself close to the x-axis in terms of introversion/extroversion. If you are either a Mission Controller/Kindred Spirit or Kindred Spirit/Mission Controller (as I am), then your introversion dominates, and you have more of a balance of the analytic and intuitive traits.

For most of us, one characteristic is more dominant than the other. Either our extroversion, introversion, analytic thinking, or intuitive thinking dominates. To reflect this, we also identify a Secondary Asking Style.

My Asking Style

Once I found out I was a Kindred Spirit/Mission Controller, it put so much in perspective for me.

I had always known that I was incredibly sensitive and feelings-oriented, and that I preferred one-on-one, deeper connections and conversations to large groups and more casual conversations. I am allergic to small talk and have had to work hard to stay focused and in the moment when the conversation is fairly light. However, I've always been able to do it well when required, and that has led people to see me as a strong, enthusiastic socializer and conversationalist. They just didn't know the effort it took.

I've also always been focused on making others feel good and on coming through for them. I demonstrate that people are important by showing up for them, complementing them, finding the perfect gift, sending personal notes, and making other important gestures. I always go along with what others want—the movie they want to see, the restaurant they want to visit, the time they want to get together. I'm the conciliator.

My feelings-oriented nature has also led me to be conflict-averse throughout my life. It has been hard not to see negotiation as criticism, or as the other party not hearing, understanding, or respecting me. And, if none of those, it has just felt awkward. Of course, this has made asking donors for gifts particularly challenging.

But I always knew I also had a strong numbers-oriented, organizer side. I was called "Brain Salad" in high school because of my math abilities, and I pursued an economics degree, a business degree, and an architecture degree. All required a lot of math, systems, logic, etc. And while I never had the interest in making personal budgets and monitoring my own finances, I was quite adept at doing so professionally.

I also finally understood why I've often ended up organizing or leading some effort or group though I truly have no desire to do so. It's because I have the skills to do it if required, and I will do it because my Kindred Spirit side would feel bad if I didn't help knowing that I could. A sense of responsibility, with a strong dose of guilt, has been a significant guide in my life.

Finding One's Asking Style

What do you think your Primary Asking Style is? Your Secondary Asking Style? I encourage you to guess, and then stop and take the quiz at quiz.askingmatters.com or scanning the QR code below with your mobile device:

It only takes three minutes to answer the 30 true/false questions, and you'll get an immediate result, which includes not only your Primary Asking Style but your Secondary Style. You can take the quiz on all your devices.

If you stopped to take it, what are your thoughts? Some people say, "You nailed me." Others are surprised but see how the result makes sense. Some are still on the fence, and that could very well mean you're close to the middle of the graph—extremely balanced in these key attributes.

VOICES FROM THE FIELD

ANDREA KIHLSTEDT (Go-Getter/Rainmaker)
Co-Founder, Capital Campaign Pro

Brian Saber and I had known one another for some years before we got together to create Asking Matters. I had been his consultant on a large and successful capital campaign. And our working relationship was terrific.

I liked the way he worked. He was principled and super aware of the feelings of people around him. He was flexible in his thinking and could flow as the situation changed, making the most of the opportunities on hand.

He was in charge, and I was his consultant. Our relationship worked well.

A couple of years later, when both of our lives had changed, we got together and decided to create Asking Matters—a business based on an idea I had long been toying with, Asking Styles.

We created a partnership and started a business together. As we fleshed out the idea of Asking Styles, Brian and I realized that our styles were different. While we were both deeply intuitive in our thinking, I was a strong extrovert, and he was a strong introvert.

I was the first person to be labeled a Go-Getter and Brian was the first to assume the label of Kindred Spirit!

We both enjoyed the free-flowing thinking of intuitive people, but our needs for reflection and time to regroup were very different. The more we talked, the more excited I would get. And the more excited I'd get, the more I'd talk.

But for Brian, a bit of wonderful free-flowing talk and ideas went a very long way. It wouldn't take long before he needed mental space. I'd get more loquacious, and he'd get quieter.

And, because Brian's a strong Kindred Spirit, he didn't say "Shut up, Kihlstedt, I've had enough for now." No, he'd just go quiet, and I wouldn't even notice.

We'd finish our meeting, I thinking we had had a great session and Brian feeling as though he'd been run over by a bulldozer. I needed to recognize my tendency to go on and how that might affect Brian, and Brian needed to recognize my brainstorming was just that and make clear what his limits were. Needless to say, those meetings went downhill over time!

Only now are we able to acknowledge and laugh about our differences—to see and understand that our different styles created a strong and effective relationship. All I needed was to recognize that when Brian got quiet, it wasn't because he loved what I was saying. It was because he felt flattened. And Brian had to learn that I wasn't trying to roll over him; I was just high on my ideas.

For all of you Go-Getters out there, remember this. We are drawn to Kindred Spirits. They flow with us for a while and give us the space to let our ideas sail. But if we don't stay aware of our bulldozing tendencies, we'll run people over without knowing it.

Even while you're having fun with the flow, remember that when your Kindred Spirit counterpart gets quiet, it's time for you to ask what's going on with them.

Chapter Five

Leading Up to
The Meeting

Now that you hopefully have your Asking Style at hand, let's talk about everything that leads up to that first meeting.

Selecting Prospects

As with dating, not everyone's an ideal match. If you're a major gifts officer, you may have no choice in who you cultivate and solicit. You might be responsible for a portfolio, a region, or some other bucket of donors. This could also be true if you're the executive director of a small organization, as I was back in the late

1980s. In that role, I had to cultivate and solicit everyone, though I could marshal board members to partner with me where helpful.

However, in many organizations there is wiggle room. Donors can be assigned based on relationship or expected compatibility. Staff and volunteers can partner with each other (more on that later). Donors can move up and down the "hot list" based on how effective a fundraiser thinks they can be in building that relationship. And, certainly with board members, we benefit from giving them wide latitude in terms of who they cultivate and possibly solicit. For if we have them work with prospects they are loath to approach, we risk them doing the work begrudgingly and frustratingly, if at all.

The Asking Styles are a useful lens into these dynamics. Let's see how they impact who introverts are most comfortable cultivating and soliciting, and how they shape the overall dynamic with various donors.

Though donors aren't, in this relationship, asking, they themselves still have an Asking Style. We'll talk at length about donors and introversion in Chapter 7, but it's important to touch on it here. Donors are still Rainmakers, Go-Getters, Kindred Spirits or Mission Controllers. Understanding your Style in relationship to theirs will give you a strong sense of who might be the best match for you to cultivate and, hopefully, solicit, and what the dynamic between you could be.

As a Kindred Spirit, I've always found Rainmaker donors the most challenging. They can intimidate me with their line of questioning and their driven nature. They come on strong, which can cause me to pull back and get cautious. If I have a choice, I'm happy to let someone else take the lead with Rainmakers.

I semi-jokingly say I love Go-Getters until they drive me crazy. Their enthusiasm is infectious, but sometimes they pull me into an uncomfortable zone, as Andrea spoke about in the last chapter. Mission Controller fundraisers can be particularly challenged by Go-Getters. While a Mission Controller fundraiser is working hard to lead the meeting systematically, the Go-Getter donor is heading in various directions as the mood strikes them. Questions can come out of left field. Important questions for sure, but questions that throw off the Mission Controller.

Not surprisingly, I find it easiest to build a relationship with my fellow Kindred Spirits. In life in general, while the expression "opposites attract" might be true, in fact we often get along best with those with a similar temperament or personality to ours. We speak a similar language and evaluate things similarly. We have a similar rhythm. Further, people generally like having their views validated, and hanging around with those who share them, at least socially and interactively, is comforting and edifying. Of course, we know there can be a downside to this, but that's for another book!

In addition to generally looking at how your Style and the Style of your donor match up, which we will explore further in Chapter 7, I have found that different Asking Styles are drawn to different categories of donors. I find this concept particularly helpful for board members. In general, board members will not have the fundraising training or experience that staff have. To the extent board members can be paired with donors they inherently find it easier to cultivate and possibly solicit, it increases the odds of them doing the work and doing it well.

For my fellow Kindred Spirit board members, I highly recommend steering clear of your closest connections, as it's all personal for us and any rejection will really hurt. Instead, focus on the low-hanging fruit, such as other board members and the organization's longstanding donors. Start with the donors most likely to be receptive and to say "yes" to help you build your confidence. No one likes rejection but it's hardest on Kindred Spirits, who will take it the most personally.

Our other introverts, the Mission Controllers, will systematically and more objectively (analytically) reach out to their networks. Given their objective nature it will be easier for them to reach out to people they know well. They will come up with a plan and work their way through their list over time.

I am also likely to ask Mission Controller board members to help with family foundations. Family foundations are a good fit because even though the money is in many ways still an individual's or family's own money, they've created a more formal structure for it. Chances are the foundation has giving guidelines, deadlines, requests for proposals and/or reports, and such. Working with these parameters takes advantage of the Mission Controller's planful and systematic nature.

Having said all this, often a volunteer will, for one reason or another, cultivate and solicit a donor whose Style is challenging given theirs. In that case, understanding in advance the dynamic that could arise given each other's Style will allow the volunteer to prepare themself for that conversation. For example, if as a Kindred Spirit I do sit down with a Rainmaker donor, I'm sure to bring along data-driven reports. I might not automatically present them, but for sure I want them handy as my Rainmaker donor may very well ask for them.

The Cultivation Process

Much of the individual donor cultivation process is tailor-fitted to us introverts as we much prefer one-to-one interactions to big group activities, and in fact much cultivation is not accomplished through group activities—or at least shouldn't be.

Of course, there are group activities that are excellent cultivation opportunities, and we introverts must embrace them. These include celebrations of the organization, opportunities to see a program in action or participate in it, volunteer opportunities, thank you and recognition events, and so forth.

Yet, if we're going to cultivate anyone for anything significant—to make a large gift, to take on a leadership volunteer position, or to open the door to someone else, just to name three—success will be based on getting to know the donor personally and individually. It will be based on a rich one-to-one conversation where we can find out the donor's interests and they can get their questions answered. This almost always happens in more intimate one-on-one or small-group settings.

These conversations, ideally, take place in person. That will always be the gold standard, but it's never been possible 100% of the time for a host of reasons, from time constraints to logistics to the donor's wishes. It used to be that phone was the next best option, but now we've got video chatting. This is a good thing, as introverts generally are not fans of the phone. We'll talk more about that later in this chapter in terms of setting up meetings.

If we're lucky, we meet with our donors a few times a year. Even if we can meet three or four times, which is rare, what happens in between is extremely important. And here is another area where introverts have the edge.

We introverts prefer to write rather than use the phone, and in the age of email, this works significantly to our benefit. Whereas in a conversation we often speed up our thought process to speak in the rhythm of the conversation, in an email exchange we are free to take our time to carefully write out our thoughts.

When our donor emails us a question, we can think through the answer fully before responding. When we have something to say, we can craft it and send it out when it feels done. (Mission Controllers—make sure not to overthink your emails and fear pushing the send button.)

Further, introverts are more likely to keep their donors in mind. Kindred Spirits, in their quest for everyone to always be happy with us, will continuously wonder what they can do to make their donors feel good. They tend to check in and make gestures at random moments, which have a particularly genuine feel to them. The fact that these gestures are unexpected catches the donor by surprise, and that has an impact.

Mission Controllers are great at planning out their donor interactions. So, while those efforts may not be as spontaneous as those of Kindred Spirits, they are meaningful and regular. It's unlikely a Mission Controller's donors will go too long without hearing from them.

Setting Up Meetings

For ages I've been told that I should just pick up the phone when I want to speak to a donor, even just to set up a meeting. For ages I've said no way! I have never liked the phone and probably would have given up fundraising if email hadn't come into play 30 or so years ago. It's been a lifesaver.

Asking introverts to call someone, especially out of the blue, is asking for something challenging. Asking them to call someone they don't even know can be torturous. Forty years ago, I was a college student phonathoner. I'd call alums and ask for gifts. I hated it and swore I wouldn't do it again...and I haven't!

Putting aside all the issues inherent in fundraising—fear of rejection, not knowing how to negotiate, etc.—the idea of the call itself gives me angst. Besides a few close friends and family, I find calling just about anyone else out of the blue difficult. There are two reasons.

First—and this is across the board—I worry the call won't be well-received and it'll be awkward. Perhaps someone will be busy and only pick it up because it's me, but then want to rush the call to conclusion. Or, specifically with a donor, perhaps they won't pick up but someone else will, and then I'll be left explaining things to a suspicious spouse or significant other, or a puzzled child.

Second, I find it so hard to read the conversation without a face and body language to scan. The eyes, the smile, the posture— they're all huge clues for me as to how someone is feeling. I can't read the voice in and of itself.

My rule of thumb for fundraisers is to reach out in the way that's most comfortable for you, all things considered. For most introverts, that's going to be in writing. Today that's generally email, though with donors you know very well, a text can also be appropriate. The idea of a formal mailed letter followed by a call is becoming more and more archaic.

Of course, if you know your donor and their preference is the phone, you might have to call. They may have told you to do so, explaining they don't like or check email. And if you've tried to contact your donor by email more than twice without a response, you might have to switch your technique and resort to the phone in order to reach them.

But, if you're like me, you'll always find writing a bit more comfortable. With writing you've eliminated the unknown of how they'll act in the moment...and how you'll respond when you're on the spot.

One last point here on donor preference, which we'll touch on again in our chapter on introverted donors. Since half of your donors, statistically, will be introverts themselves, keep in mind that many of them could find a call intrusive. They might prefer written communication, just like introverted fundraisers. They might prefer to consider your request to find a time to meet without the pressure of giving you a response on the spot. Given that, the advice that one should always call doesn't make sense half the time.

Preparing for Meetings

How do introverts prepare for meetings with donors? We can talk about some ideal of getting every bit of information you can possibly get, including biographical information, history of giving to your organization and elsewhere, financials, and more. And chances are Mission Controllers will strive to gather the most information of anyone.

But then there are the realities. First, we have just so much time, and if we spend endless time researching we'll never get out the door (analysis paralysis). Second, no matter how much research we do we can't learn everything on our own; there's much that only our donors can tell us. Third, not everything we learn second or thirdhand is accurate.

So our reality is that we get what we can in advance, and we plan to learn a lot in the meetings themselves. Further, if we're meeting a donor for the first time and it's for a cultivation meeting, preparation can be as much about us feeling comfortable with the unknown as it is knowing about the donor.

This comfort often comes from having some sort of road map for the meeting. We'll discuss a powerful framework for meetings in the next chapter, and at the root of it is asking revealing questions. Developing those questions in advance is a great strength of introverts.

As a Kindred Spirit, over the years I found if I wrote down a series of questions in advance, I could recall them in the moment rather than having to create them on the spot. Of course, this aligns with what we now know about introverts and our neurotransmitters. Given the depth at which we think and how we rely less on short-term memory, taking the time in advance to prepare questions makes sense.

This preparation has been particularly helpful to me for questions I might ask early on in a conversation as I'm settling into the meeting. Unless I know a donor well and have a comfortable relationship already, the beginning of a meeting is challenging for me. It takes a few minutes for me to get into a groove.

By the way, as an intuitive I'm not heavy on research, but I do make sure to know what a donor would expect me to know, namely their prior relationship with the organization and their personal connections to it. Depending on how visible they are in the community or the world, they'd also expect me to know about them professionally, etc. If a board member or someone else I know has a connection to the donor, I will ask them for background information. And, of course, I'll research them on Google, Facebook, and LinkedIn.

Mission Controllers will plan out their meetings in much more detail, practically writing a script. This can be very helpful, as long as you understand that a meeting will often go in an unplanned direction and it's important to be nimble in the moment. That can challenge Mission Controllers, who do everything to avoid surprises and can find it tough to be flexible in the moment. To avoid that challenge, and the pregnant pause that might accompany something you're not expecting, it will help to think through possible responses to your questions and how you might respond in kind.

A word on role plays as preparation since I get asked about them all the time. We introverts tend to hate them. I cringe at the thought. I'd much rather prepare on my own, or by chatting with a team member, than have to act out some hypothetical scenario. In a formal training I find it even more cringeworthy as others might be watching me. All to say that you should prepare in the way that suits you best, as that's the way you are most likely to prepare well.

Now it's time to meet.

Chapter Six

Conducting the Meeting... and Following Through

At Asking Matters we use the Arc of the Ask, developed by Andrea Kihlstedt herself, to ensure that all our conversations are intentional. Let's use it here to understand introverted fundraisers' strengths and challenges in a meeting and beyond.

Whether we're asking for a cash gift, volunteer support, an introduction to others, board involvement, etc., every meeting has a similar arc. We're always asking for something in a meeting, even if it's just asking whether we can send some information or follow up in a month. So, while the Arc of the Ask was specifically developed for solicitation meetings, most of what it conveys will help you navigate any meeting.

Settling: Those Opening Moments

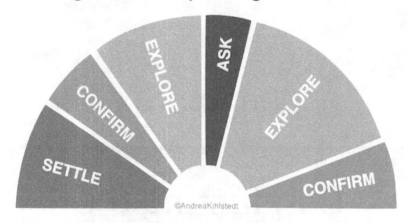

The opening minutes of any meeting are crucial. We're now either in the same space physically, looking at each other via video chat, or listening to each other by phone, and it's important to settle in and get on the same wavelength emotionally. So much trust and goodwill depend on those first few minutes, and it's also a key moment to learn personal facts about our donor.

It's a great opportunity to ask our donor about their family, their work, what they did this past weekend, and more. If we were introduced through a third party, it's the time to underscore the relationship and talk briefly about that person. If we're in someone's work or home office, we can ask about on-site vs. remote work. If we've had conversations before, this is the time to follow up on what we learned last time. *How was that vacation? How did your daughter's college search go? How is the new home or job?*

As an introvert, I always find the first few minutes of a solicitation meeting challenging. In fact, I find the first few minutes of any meeting or gathering challenging. I need those first moments to gather my thoughts, get a read on the other participants, and become accustomed to the environment. Yet those are the moments when the conversation is most likely to be free-flowing and random, calling on those short-term memory abilities that can challenge introverts.

If I know a donor well, that's helpful, as there's already some rapport and I have a better sense of what to expect from our interaction. However, as we discussed earlier, more often than not we're meeting with someone we don't know particularly well. That creates extra anxiety for me and my fellow introverts. Just as we need more time than usual to get in a groove, we're in a situation where we're expected to be more fluid and spontaneous.

To counter this, ideally we bring along an extroverted asking partner (a Rainmaker or Go-Getter) who can get the meeting started while we survey the situation and acclimate. And if our partner is someone who knows the donor better than we do, it's a double benefit as it's natural for our partner and the donor to start off the conversation.

Short of having that extroverted partner available, the list of opening questions we discussed in the last chapter helps us greatly in these moments.

Confirming

This is a quick step during which we confirm the purpose of the meeting and the amount of time we have. This makes sure we're on the same page and there are no surprises, either on the donor's part (being surprised we're asking for a gift, if that's the purpose of our meeting) or our part (the donor lets us know late in the meeting that they have to leave early and we haven't covered everything yet).

Mission Controllers, in particular, excel here. They are great at following plans and appreciate the system of the Arc of the Ask. They also understand the importance of taking this step as a means of dotting their i's and crossing their t's.

Kindred Spirits will be less enthusiastic about confirming the purpose of the meeting, especially if it's an ask for a gift, as it feeds into their concern for possible confrontation or even just run-of-the-mill awkwardness. However, they'll gladly confirm the timing of the meeting in order to cater to their donors' time constraints.

Exploring

A well-run meeting is full of exploration. In addition to the opening personal questions, much time is spent exploring your donor's relationship to the organization and to philanthropy. What does the donor think of your organization? Are there particular programs they find most appealing? What are they trying to accomplish philanthropically? If they've given before, what prompted those gifts, and how do they feel about having made them?

How do my fellow introverts navigate this exploration? Rather well, in fact.

My fellow Kindred Spirits might be thinking, "Oh, no—I've got to ask all these questions? That feels so intrusive." But that'll be countered by, "At least I can talk less and listen more—that sounds appealing." And, as we discussed in Chapter 3, the less you talk and the more you listen, the more you'll learn.

Yet Kindred Spirits can look at it from another angle. Asking questions puts the donor front and center. It's a way of showing that we're paying attention, that we're interested, and that it's important to us to know more—not just close a gift. And since attending to others and making them feel heard and important is key to a Kindred Spirit's personality, by doing that, we're being true to ourselves.

Using my romantic history as a parallel, I have always asked my dates lots of questions. I am naturally curious about people, but I also want them to feel I'm paying attention and am interested in them. I can keep any conversation going, even when it seems I'm pulling teeth. Fascinatingly, I can ask ten questions in a row without being asked one back. Sometimes, when I truly tire of asking questions and allow for a pregnant pause in the conversation, my date will say, "Now tell me about you." I try, without being snarky, to say, "Well, ask me a question. I'm an open book!"

Mission Controllers find exploration even easier. Chances are you Mission Controllers have an outline, a script, a list of questions, or some other framework, and you're very happy to systematically move through your questions, sitting back quietly in between. Further, your interest in research will lead you to ask interesting follow-up questions, which help you dig deeper.

By the way, these explorations can be challenging for extroverts, though at first one might think otherwise. Rainmakers aren't big on process, so they won't naturally ask a lot of questions and might very well be wondering how quickly they can get to the ask. Though in fact the goal is not the ask but how well the meeting moves the relationship ahead, Rainmakers find it hard to evaluate their progress if there hasn't been a quantitative, measurable success.

Go-Getters tend to talk more, asking fewer questions and listening less, so they are likely to learn far less about their donors. And while the Rainmaker's questions (few as they might be) are strategically chosen and tend to bring important information to light, a

Go-Getter's questions can sometimes be wide of the mark as new ideas and lines of conversation come to mind.

Segueing: Moving on to Our Story And the Ask

I always say there are three moments in the conversation that tend to be most challenging. The first is segueing to our story. The second is the actual ask, and the third is being quiet after the ask; we'll discuss those two shortly.

Segueing involves acknowledging what we've learned and telling our story about the organization. Perhaps it starts something like this:

> "Thank you so much for sharing why you care about Allendale Senior Center and helping me better understand what's important to you in choosing charities to support. Your comments about touching the mission resonated deeply with me as it was my volunteer work with the Center that cemented my passion for it and brought me to the board. As a board member I've gotten to understand the ins and outs of the Center and I have been deeply touched by the progress we've made in minimizing loneliness in the folks we serve..."

The ideal time to segue to the ask is somewhere in the middle of the meeting, after much exploration about our donor's relationship to the organization and philanthropy, but not so late in the meeting that there won't be time to explore the donor's response to our request. Sensing when that moment has arrived is challenging. Some meetings are so rich in conversation that it makes sense to extend the exploration. Other times it's like pulling teeth to get our donor to talk, and we may very well find ourselves out of questions early on. And even if it feels like the right time, segueing can still feel like an abrupt change of course.

Everyone finds this moment of turning the conversation, to our story and the ask, challenging. Having said that, our Mission Controllers generally do this best. You've planned for this moment and, when the time comes, you will take the next step because that's the plan. Your challenge comes when the plan has been upended. It's hard for Mission Controllers to deviate from the plan, as you might have to if the conversation has died earlier than expected, or if it's going strong and should continue longer. Try not to force the conversation one way or the other.

Our other introverts, the Kindred Spirits, will find this moment harder. My fellow Kindred Spirits will relate to my general sense of anxiety at this moment, which comes from our issues with confrontation. Now, of course, the ask isn't a confrontational moment, but since we take everything personally and hate negotiation, we can mistakenly see what will follow as confrontational. What's the best way to avoid confrontation? Stall as long as possible! So Kindred Spirits often put off segueing to their story and the ask.

At the end of the day, I think what keeps me on track most here is my deep-seated need, as a Kindred Spirit, to please everyone else. I simply must do the right thing and come through for my organization, my boss, my peers, whomever. I know it's up to me to do this right or possibly leave money on the table, so I forge ahead, queueing up the request with the appropriate segue.

The Ask

Not to diminish how hard it can be, but the ask itself is but a moment in time. Best practice is to ask for an exact amount, and in this manner: "Would you consider a gift of $10,000 to the Center this year?" While we can't dissect fully in this book why this is best practice, I would like to make two points.

The first is that "Would you consider" is very open, inviting, and conditional, so it allows the donor to come forward and consider the request. Most people, if we ask whether they'd consider something, will do so if it's at all in the realm of possibility and sounds reasonable. We ask for an exact amount because our donors are generally expecting it, as we've asked them if we can meet to talk about a gift. They assume we've got something in mind and are waiting to hear what that amount is. In fact, often a donor has said to me, "I know you've got something in mind—what did you want to ask me for?"

Everyone is challenged at this moment. No matter how confident one is, this is still the moment of truth, and the answer is out of your control. I'll continue my pattern of pointing to the Mission Controller's understanding, at this moment, of the importance of the system, and the Kindred Spirit's desire to come through and do what's expected. However, what I hope you will embrace most is that as long as you say the right words, even if you fumble over them a bit, appear reticent or apologetic, rush through them, or whatever—you're fine.

Because of my success closing gifts, people assume I have some special skill, especially at this moment of reckoning. In fact, I don't. After decades in the business, I can still stumble over my words now and again, and I've been known to blush. The truth is—or should be—that the ask is in many ways the least important moment. If we've done our work cultivating our donor, and we've had a rich conversation in this meeting, our donor will be primed for our ask. As long as we get it out, we're okay. Seriously.

Does this mean doing it with confidence and conviction doesn't help? Of course not; it does help—but it helps less than one might think. Almost everyone I've asked has already been on our side— the side of the organization. They've wanted to come through for the organization...and sometimes for me, as people do give to people. They've been waiting to hear what amount I have in mind so they can respond, and what they're focused on is the amount. How we couch the ask is critical, but how the words come out is not. I truly believe that.

The Third Challenge

As challenging as it can be to ask for the gift (and at the right time), it's often just as challenging to keep silent after we've asked. Those five seconds—and it's rarely more than that—can feel like an eternity, right?! This moment reminds me of the moment when a check comes to the table at the end of a donor meeting. Our hope is the donor will pick it up, seeing it as part of their support of the institution. But we can only wait five seconds before grabbing the check ourselves.

Here's where the Mission Controller's love of following instructions comes in handy. If you've been taught that being silent until the donor talks is best practice, you'll gladly follow that best practice. Also, as the best listener in the group, you'll be glad that your time to talk is over and you can now sit back and listen.

Kindred Spirits will be relieved that they've gotten the ask out, and that the next move is the donor's. However, you might go on if you're anxious, filling the silence while the donor is still processing the request. And this is why, for thirty years, my number one prop has been a beverage.

I make every effort to have something to drink, even just a

glass of water, by my side. As soon as I've asked the donor to consider a particular gift, I raise the glass and take a sip. Try it now. It takes about five seconds to reach for it, pick it up, take a sip, and put it back down. And virtually every time, in those five seconds, your donor will respond. Remember, you're having a conversation, so the next "move" is your donor's. It's in the hands of the donor to respond...however long it takes.

I wish I could remember who taught me this back in my early days of fundraising, as it's one of the most valuable tips I ever received. I think it's valuable for everyone, but perhaps most for us Kindred Spirits (and you talkative Go-Getters!)

Exploring Post-Ask

Now we've asked for something and gotten a response. It might be an outright "Sure, yes, I'll do that." But, more often than not, we'll hear something more qualified. A donor might express interest but have questions. Or say they need time to think about it. They might have a concern about the amount, the timing, or the proposed use of the funds.

We ask in the middle of the meeting to leave time to explore our donor's response, as we learn as much if not more from this discussion as we did earlier in the meeting. In fact, I believe there is much we don't learn until we ask for a gift, especially when we've asked for a specific amount. It is often only at this point that we hear directly from the donor about their capacity, their other financial commitments, their charitable priorities and, last but not least, how close to our organization they feel.

All the data in the world can't give us this full picture, which is a particular frustration for Mission Controllers. You head into the meeting with tons of information, yet often there is a piece missing. Living with this ambiguity is difficult but important.

There's no question that good, active listening is paramount at this post-ask moment. Otherwise, it's easy to over-interpret what the donor is saying, jump to a conclusion, and blurt something out that misses the point. Hearing the donor's response and digesting it before responding gives us those few seconds to fully grasp the donor's message. This is an area of strength for introverts and challenge for extroverts, especially Go-Getters. While extroverts might feel confident in their response as they talk to think, I've seen many extroverts respond too quickly and miss the point the donor was making.

Kindred Spirits will excel at sympathizing with the donor's questions or concerns, helping the donor feel heard and appreciated. Kindred Spirits might even, at this juncture, share a relevant personal story or experience to help value what the donor is saying. It will be clear to the donor that the Kindred Spirit has heard them.

However, given a Kindred Spirit's tendency to avoid confrontation and our sense that all negotiation feels like confrontation, it will be difficult for us to ask further questions. We can see delving into the donor's concerns as a bit pushy, perhaps even an invasion of privacy. That can't be further from the truth if we work to see asking questions through the donor's eyes. Asking questions shows we care about our donor. That we're trying to fully understand their agenda so we can help fulfill it. And that our request was important in the first place.

Mission Controllers will excel at listening and asking follow-up questions. You will systematically try to glean more information and fill in the blanks. One caution for Mission Controllers is the tendency to give too much detail. Listen closely to what your donor is asking and don't over-deliver the answer. Keep in mind that your donor can only remember so much anyway...and they can always ask another question.

Confirming Post-Ask

As the meeting comes to a close, it's the fundraiser's role to confirm what has transpired and what the next steps will be. Again, Mission Controllers excel at dotting the i's and crossing the t's. Kindred Spirits might feel a bit reticent reiterating the donor's intentions and everyone's next steps, but it's important to leave with a clear understanding all around.

Here's a tip: Always put the next step in your court. Even if the donor offers to get back to you, take that task off their list and say you'll follow up on a certain, agreed-to date. This eliminates the awkwardness of awaiting a donor's response that doesn't come when expected.

Following Through

I always email my donor the same day we've met. I want to let the donor know how much I appreciated the meeting, and I want to confirm the details while the conversation is fresh. This eliminates one or the other side moving ahead with any misconceptions.

Both Styles, as lovers of email, will do a fine job of following up immediately to confirm next steps in writing. I've always found this a key step in the process, one that extroverts can find bothersome: Rainmakers aren't big on process and will want to move onto something else, and Go-Getters might rush through the step. Introverts are more likely to get it right. Mission Controllers will cover all the bases clearly, including writing detailed contact reports, and Kindred Spirits will write the donor something warm and fuzzy. A combination of the two will serve you best.

Chapter Seven

Embracing Our
Introverted Donors

One of those great "aha" moments for me came a few years into developing the Asking Styles, when a participant in one of my trainings asked me if the donor's personality impacted how we looked at the Styles. Duh! I couldn't believe we hadn't focused on that previously.

Identifying Introverted Donors

Of course, the first question is how to identify an introverted donor. Wouldn't it be great if we could ask our donors to take the

Asking Styles Quiz or provide some documentation from some other personality test before we ever communicate with them? Short of that, there are ways to get a strong sense of whether our donor might be an introvert or not.

Sometimes I make a guess as to someone's Asking Style and introversion based on their profession. Lawyers, scientists, writers, and others of similar professions tend to fall into the Mission Controller (analytic introvert) quadrant. Therapists, nurses, and others in helping professions often are found in the intuitive-introvert Kindred Spirit quadrant. Obviously, none of this is set in stone, but there are strong patterns linking certain professions to certain Styles.

Special events can give you a clue as well. Though we'll talk about special events at length in Chapter 10, suffice it to say that we're not seeing many of our introverted donors at our special events. Thinking back to our conversation about dopamine, which is less active in introverts, it means they don't get the same rush from being at events with lots of people that the extroverts do.

If our introverted donors do attend, we won't find them working the room. We're more likely to find them in quiet conversation off to the side or at a table. And they'll be the first to leave. How often have I wondered, upon entering some larger event, how early it would be appropriate to leave.

Introverts are the most likely to send their regrets, perhaps with a gift. Which of your donors regularly contribute in lieu of attending? That could be a sign that they're introverts.

Even more telling is how our introverted donors reach out to us. My introverted donors rarely phone me when they've got a question, because it's just as awkward for introverts to be on either end of a surprise conversation. Email has been a true friend to introverted donors, who are much more likely to ask a question or report a concern if they can do so in writing.

And when we call an introverted donor out of the blue to set up a meeting, we are likely to put that donor in an awkward position. While the element of surprise might work for some, it will not work for the introvert, who is now on the spot to respond in the moment, without the time we've established is necessary for the introvert to fully process the question.

Is that what we want? I don't think so. It's hard enough doing this work without creating additional barriers. Given that, as noted earlier, it amazes me that anyone still thinks it's best practice to just pick up the phone and call. It might be if you're calling an extrovert, or someone you know very well, but it just as often is not best practice. So why not do what you do best?

I'd go as far to say that email has given us much more access to introverted donors, and we should take advantage of that. I noted earlier that email has been my friend. It's also been my most potent tool. I love writing warm, personal emails and having lengthy email conversations with donors. It's so much easier for me, and I sense it is for most of our donors today, even the extroverted ones, as cell phones, spam calls, and texting have made the phone a minefield for many.

By the way, I don't think an introverted donor, when I've run across them somewhere, has ever said "Call me sometime." They're likely to ask me to email them. I rarely tell anyone but my dearest friends, in fact, to "Call me sometime." I would encourage someone to email me. I might ask them to text me. But call me? No way.

A note here. In no way am I saying that email should be used in lieu of a meeting when discussing a gift. Email is great for setting up meetings, updating donors on your organization's activities, sharing great stories, and reminding them about upcoming events, end-of-year deadlines, and such. But nothing compares to an in-person meeting, and the fallback should now be a video chat. A phone call becomes a distant third option. But not email. I have discussed and closed gifts by email, but that can only be at the donor's behest, and with no alternative.

The fact that we have introverted donors is another reason why we introverts are such important fundraisers. As we established earlier, somewhere around 50% of our donors are introverts. If we accept the fact that we often are attracted to people similar to ourselves, we can immediately picture an introverted donor being more at ease with an introverted fundraiser and vice versa. For one, we'll both enjoy not talking to each other on the phone! We'll start a rich email conversation instead.

What Motivates Them to Meet

As we explore the relationship with introverted donors, we come to understand that the one-on-one donor meetings we crave with all donors are also in the sweet spot for introverted donors. The same donors who will turn down big fundraising events and group cultivation events will be much more inclined to accept a private invitation to meet. That meeting could be in someone's home or at their office, or ideally to see programming in action, live and firsthand.

We can also start to understand what motivates our introverted donors to meet. Kindred Spirits might well meet because we asked them to, and they want to come through for us. They might feel bad about the prospect of rejecting our request. However, they are also the most likely to say they don't want us going out of our way, and we'll have to convince them it's absolutely no bother. So much will be based on the connection we've formed, or at least on the friendly, personable way we approach them.

Mission Controller donors will meet because they understand that's the system for fundraising, and because they're wired to learn as much as they can about our organization. That information builds their trust and gets them excited. Wanting to be prepared, they'll ask us to send information in advance, or in lieu of, a meeting, and they'll devour the information and ask lots of questions when we meet or otherwise communicate.

How Meetings with Introverted Donors Unfold

When we finally do talk face-to-face, an introverted donor's Style also impacts the kinds of questions they ask, what gets discussed, and the rhythm of the conversation.

A Kindred Spirit donor will spend the most time settling into the meeting with friendly conversation. The personal connection is important to them, and they will want to know how the fundraiser is doing and what's new in their life, and will readily share the same about themself. As the conversation turns to the organization, they'll also want to know how the participants in the program are doing and will enjoy hearing lots of feel-good success stories.

Perhaps it goes without saying, at this point, that Kindred Spirit fundraisers will have an advantage here. Kindred Spirit fundraisers will tell their "heart" stories, either about specific program participants whose lives have been impacted or about how the organization has impacted them personally. Their Kindred Spirit donors will be warmed by these heart-centered stories and a common bond will build.

A Mission Controller donor will be less forthright on the personal front and will take less time to settle into the meeting. However, with a fundraiser's lead they will continue to answer the personal questions that are posed. As the conversation focuses on the work, a Mission Controller donor will have lots of questions about how your organization is doing its work. What methods are you employing, and how are they working? How do you take a participant through your program step by step? What are you planning for the future?

Again, as with two Kindred Spirits, a Mission Controller fundraiser will have an advantage with Mission Controller donors. They'll tell their "plan" stories, which will greatly appeal to Mission Controller donors. Further, they'll enjoy answering the donor's questions. For both of them, the more information the better.

Whether the donor and fundraiser share the same Style or not, if they're both introverted Styles, the conversation will feel easier. Referring back to the rhythm of a conversation and the introvert's natural tendency to think before talking, two introverts in conversation will naturally make room for each other. The introverted donor won't need to speed up their thinking to keep pace in the conversation. They won't worry that a slow response might mean the fundraiser in the conversation chimes in with something else before they can answer. They won't feel they're being peppered with questions, as the introverted fundraiser's questions will come at a slower pace.

Now imagine the challenge an extroverted fundraiser might have with an introverted donor. Imagine a Go-Getter fundraiser meeting with a Mission Controller donor. It would be very difficult for the Go-Getter to leave all that silent space in the conversation, and yet not doing so will silence the donor. Further, the Go-Getter will tend to take the conversation in many different directions, while the Mission Controller will want the conversation to unfold more linearly.

A Rainmaker fundraiser might be challenged in a different way. Tending to be short on process, they might not give enough space in the conversation for the Mission Controller donor to ask all their questions. And they might push a bit hard against the Mission Controller's innate desire to think through something slowly and purposefully.

As for Rainmaker fundraisers soliciting Kindred Spirit donors, this can also present a challenge. Rainmakers tend to come on strong. They're all business and might ask tough, strategic questions that put the Kindred Spirit on the spot. The Kindred Spirit donor might not want to answer various questions but could feel compelled in their desire to come through for the fundraiser, creating significant discomfort for the donor.

Particularly with introverted donors, Kindred Spirit fundraisers have the added benefit of their natural tendency to put people at ease. Given that fundraising discussions can be awkward for all donors—extroverted and introverted—having those attentive, caring, solicitous traits in abundance is a great advantage.

However, as natural as these conversations might be, introverted fundraisers do need to plan ahead for meetings with fellow introverts. Whereas Rainmaker and Go-Getter donors can chat to fill the space, introverted donors will wait to take the fundraiser's lead. With an introverted fundraiser, lack of planning could lead to some long silences and to a meeting pace that lacks energy.

From start to finish, knowing which of our donors are introverted, and understanding how to best cultivate, steward, and solicit those donors, is paramount to developing the deepest relationships possible.

VOICES FROM THE FIELD

DEBBIE HAMMER (*Kindred Spirit/Go-Getter*)
Director of Development
Junior Achievement of South Florida

I come from a family where everyone is very competitive and sports-oriented...and I'm not. So, whenever they were playing sports, I'd be in the field doing somersaults and picking daisies. At dinner, everyone else would be talking about who they beat at tennis, and I felt like I was in the wrong family!

What's changed most for me in fundraising, since better understanding who I am, is how I approach donors. I used to think I had to be driven to close gifts, but I no longer think in terms of closing gifts as the win. I just focus on building one-on-one relationships, which I'm good at and enjoy.

And I never ask before I feel like I have chemistry, a relationship, or a mutual understanding.

I now know I'm not less effective. I just have different strengths. And I can fundraise more confidently knowing that.

Chapter Eight

Partnering: Maximizing Our Power

I've always been a huge fan of partnering with other fundraisers on the cultivation and solicitation of donors. Partnering has many benefits, chief among them complementing each other and bringing a stronger set of overall skills to the table. Additionally, when a donor has two individual relationships to the organization, that strengthens their connection to it.

Further, since there is inevitably turnover in fundraising staff and board members, having two relationships guarantees there will be some consistency as people come and go. Last, but not least, I personally have found partnering a way to make the work less stressful and more enjoyable.

Often in smaller shops our partners are who they are, meaning we don't have much choice. As the executive director of a tiny dance company with no development staff back in the 1980's, my number one partner was the artistic director. As a director of development at other organizations, my number one partner was often my executive director or board chair.

When I headed up major gifts in the Midwest for my alma mater, Brandeis University, I had lots of partners—local alums, the president, the provost, the dean of arts and sciences, various board members, and some faculty. At Northwestern Settlement House in Chicago, I mostly had my one amazing partner—Ron Manderschied. Our story is coming up in the next chapter.

The Asking Styles can provide a sense of who an introvert's best partners might be, as well as a sense of how various partnerships might work. And, as we discussed in Chapter 7, the personality of the donor can also influence this choice.

Who Are an Introvert's Best Partners?

All things being equal, we introverts should find ourselves an extrovert as a partner. This is especially true for Kindred Spirit/Mission Controllers and Mission Controller/Kindred Spirits. While we have some balance of analytic and intuitive thinking, we could really use some extroversion. For introverts whose Secondary Asking Style is either Rainmaker or Go-Getter, bringing the extroversion might be less of a priority, but is still helpful.

When we partner with an extrovert, we get someone who is comfortable from that first moment of a meeting. Someone who can keep a conversation going when the donor is giving one-word answers. Someone who might more easily fit into the rhythm of the conversation, especially if the donor is also an extrovert.

Throughout the cultivation process, our extroverted partner can complement us well. Perhaps we introverts take on more of the written communication while we rely on the extroverts for phone calls. At special events, as we will talk about at length in Chapter 10, perhaps the extroverts work the room while we're assigned to specific donors we can talk to one-on-one.

Our ideal partner is often found diagonally across from us on the Styles chart. For Kindred Spirits, that means a Rainmaker, and for Mission Controllers, a Go-Getter. In both instances we then have the bases covered; we're assured of having a good amount of the attributes of all four Styles.

I've often said that if my buddy, Ron, who's a Go-Getter, were a Rainmaker...he'd have been ideal. He could have brought the analytic side to the table, which would have been helpful with our analytic donors. I brought a bit as my secondary is Mission Controller, but not much! So we both brought the intuitive side, and we'll talk about that further in the next chapter.

Getting yet more specific, we can look at Secondary Styles:

Your Style	Your "Ideal" Partner's Style
Kindred Spirit/Mission Controller	Rainmaker/Go-Getter
Kindred Spirit/Go-Getter	Rainmaker/Mission Controller
Mission Controller/Kindred Spirit	Go-Getter/Rainmaker
Mission Controller/Rainmaker	Go-Getter/Kindred Spirit

Once you know your Asking Style, you can begin to understand how you complement each other, what roles each of you might play, and what your challenges might be.

Chapter Nine

My Greatest Partner: Ron

When I think back on my career in fundraising, at the center of it is Ron Manderschied, a true Go-Getter if ever there was one. Passion and vision for days, unafraid to take a big leap, engaging everyone so easily. His second Asking Style is Kindred Spirit, and in hearing our story, you'll see where his Kindred Spirit took center stage.

I first met Ron on April 5, 1991. He was in search of some campaign help at Northwestern Settlement House, where he served as president/CEO.

The Settlement was in the midst of its centennial and had launched a capital campaign to mark the occasion, but it wasn't going very well and a local funder, Jill Darrow, thought I could help. So Ron hired me as the campaign consultant (I had no campaign experience, but that's another story) and we plunged in. The first campaign quickly morphed into a larger campaign when the property adjacent to the Settlement became available and the Settlement's leaders made the wise decision to buy it to enable future expansion.

The timing was tough as our core donors had already been solicited and made their commitments to a more modest campaign. Where to turn next? Fortunately, the Settlement had a unique asset that had not been tapped—a series of auxiliary boards with almost 200 women among them. These women were very active fundraisers and passionate about the Settlement, but the boards acted independently, and very few of them were known to the staff at all.

I convinced Ron that we would never figure out on our own who might be interested in supporting the campaign without getting to know them. So, we agreed that we would visit every member of every board! We hoped everyone would consider making some campaign gift, but it was not required.

What an extraordinary move this turned out to be in every way. We had more than 150 meetings over the course of a year, lining up five in a day, mostly on Chicago's North Shore. We'd have an 8am breakfast, 10am coffee, noon lunch, 2pm coffee, and 4pm coffee/tea. Sometimes we'd have multiple meetings in a row at the same coffee shop in Winnetka. Almost everyone on the boards contributed, many significantly. We raised a ton of money, and Ron and I became the Settlement's "Dynamic Duo".

Preparing to Meet

Since Ron and I are both intuitives, neither of us is the greatest preparer in the world. As my secondary style is Mission Controller, I was the more organized, but in truth we were both just winging it. At the time we seemed to get by on our earnestness. Thirty years later and having developed the Asking Styles, I now know how we really did it.

Nowadays, research is essential. To be honest, when Ron and I started out, there wasn't nearly as much of it... pre-Google, pre-Wealth Engine, pre-everything. Mostly, we had word of mouth. We'd get some information from the Settlement's various board leaders but, in general, we went into these meetings blind.

Since we had billed these as get-to-know-yous and solicitation meetings—we always said we were coming for a gift—board members didn't expect us to know them well...and that was a good thing.

As intuitives, neither of us practiced much in advance, but we had the benefit of going out together often, and we grew as a team over time. Thinking back on our meetings, I realize our compatibility included how we transported ourselves. We drove to virtually every meeting—and Ron was always behind the wheel.

This proved fortuitous, as I could put on my Secondary Style Mission Controller hat and prep both of us as Ron drove. I'd go over the giving history, the personal information, and where we might lead the conversation, so it was fresh in our minds. And we always had an agreed-to amount to request, though more on that below.

Setting Up the Meeting

What a great team we made here! We relied on my organizational skills and Ron's extroversion. I would come up with a plan of whom we needed to reach out to each day. I'd come sit in Ron's office while he made the calls. I'd call out the names and numbers and give him whatever information I had, and he'd dial for dollars!

Having Ron make the calls was a huge relief to me. As I've already noted, I hate the phone, and I find it particularly unnerving to call people I don't know. Go-Getter Ron enjoys the phone and uses it to great advantage. Over the 30 years we worked together I often found him on the phone when I walked into his office. He could be talking with an elected official, a board member, a parent from the community, or a fellow staff member. Me? If I were in Ron's shoes, I'd be sending endless emails and hoping we could resolve things without resorting to the phone.

Settling

I was very lucky to have Ron to open the meeting. As a Go-Getter, he was much more at ease in these situations, especially when neither of us knew the donor much, if at all. Though I can be a great conversationalist once I'm in my groove, I really find meeting new people anxiety-provoking. Knowing that Ron would open the meeting and give me some time to get my footing was very helpful.

Confirming

This was always my role. I'd thank the donor for meeting with us to discuss a gift. I was always able to be more direct than Ron, and I attribute that to my Mission Controller Secondary Asking Style, not to mention I was hired to do this. Go-Getter Ron always found the business part a bit awkward—if he even remembered we had to get there. He was always in the moment, enjoying the conversation...and I envied him for that.

Exploring

We shared the exploration evenly. When the donor had program questions, Ron took most of those. The Settlement's future came from his extraordinary vision, and he was incredibly articulate and passionate about it. I always loved listening to him talk.

The questions about the campaign came to me. I'd explain where we were, what we had accomplished, and what our goals were. I was better about asking the donors questions to learn about them. Ron was always amazed at how much I could learn, but that was easy for me as my Kindred Spirit knew it would make the donors feel good. I also tend to be an open book about myself, and that helped donors be open about themselves as well.

Wearing my Secondary Style of Mission Controller, I was the conductor, meaning it was my role to keep moving the meeting along. As Ron would fully acknowledge, he tended to run long... really long! He could talk a blue streak about the Settlement, and though he was always fascinating and conveyed his unbridled enthusiasm and commitment to the institution, he tended to share too much information in the moment.

It was my job to save the donor from information overload —— the wall of words—and get to the $64,000 question. I also had to ask the key questions about the donors' philanthropy and how they felt about the Settlement because Ron wasn't a prober.

To help me control Ron's tendencies, it helped if we sat next to each other as I could kick him under the table when we ran long. If we were apart, I'd give him a look he came to read over time as "You've got to stop talking!" Worst case, I'd say, "Ron, we love hearing you talk about the Settlement, but we really do need to move on as Carole and John don't have all day."

The Ask

One hundred percent of the time over all those years, I made the ask. Trust me, I never wanted to do it! As we've established, as a Kindred Spirit I am way too feelings-oriented and conflict-averse to enjoy the role. However, it was my job and, as we established earlier, I wasn't going to let Ron and the organization down.

Also, in truth, Ron basically told me I had to do it! Sometimes he'd even tell our donors that I was going to ask as he couldn't... and that's why he brought me along! That usually got a chuckle and took some of the tension out of the room. Spoiler alert: In spite of these protestations, Ron became a superb fundraiser through our work together and went on to ask for many seven-figure gifts on his own.

As I've mentioned, people often think I had some secret sauce all these years. Some amazing technique that landed us the biggest gift possible in the moment. And I often say I don't believe I always got the biggest gift possible. I didn't have some amazing technique that left no possible response but "Sure." My success was simply in doing it. In asking for the gift in the right way...and at the right time. I simply pushed through my fears and blurted it out.

Exploring Post-Ask

This is where we would have benefited from a Rainmaker! And here's where Ron's Kindred Spirit really came out.

Ron and I were always relieved when donors were positively inclined, simply saying they needed time to think about our request. And this did happen a good deal of the time. Other times, they had questions about how the campaign was coming along, or what their payment options were.

But sometimes their initial response was about the amount of the request. If someone countered with a lower amount, it was in Ron's nature to simply accept that amount and thank the donor. As the professional fundraiser, I knew that their first offer was just that, and it was up to us to see if there was a way to get them to consider more. And though I was a confrontation/rejection-avoidant introvert, it was left to me to have that conversation...while Ron sat there cringing at the thought we might be pushing too hard. Not an easy role at all, but I always kept in mind another great Jerry Panas quote—"If you get the meeting, you are 85% of the way to getting the gift."

Confirming

It was also my role to wrap up (using my Mission Controller). I'd confirm the next steps all parties would take and when we'd make contact again. I always knew, even from our earliest days, to make sure the next contact was in our hands. It was up to Ron to call back in two weeks, or whatever the timeframe was that the donor suggested.

That was the Ron and Brian Show...and you know what? We succeeded just about every time. Back then, in the early years, I didn't know exactly why we were so successful. In some ways it took Asking Matters and deeply analyzing the ask to understand why we did so well, but certainly at the top was that we were authentic. The donors appreciated us for what we were and what we were not. Ron was his genuine Go-Getter self, and I was my genuine Kindred Spirit self. Neither of us was the stereotype of a fundraiser, and neither of us tried to be. We embraced ourselves for who we were.

Ron and I worked together for thirty years until his retirement in 2021 (in honor of which we raised $800,000!). We ran five campaigns together. Most importantly, we partnered on at least a thousand meetings with individual donors. Not only did we raise a lot of money and hone our skills, but we became dear friends.

Chapter Ten

Introverts and Special Events

M ost of this book talks about building relationships with individuals in the pursuit of "major" gifts since so much money, and so many of the biggest gifts, come from the one-to-one cultivation and solicitation of individuals. We also talk about it because we naturally think about these interactions when imagining the supposed challenges introverts might face. Now, in Chapters 10 and 11, let's look at some of the other pieces of the fundraising portfolio.

Well, we must start with special events, right? And there's no better place to start than by telling another personal story.

Personal Story II

Every year my dear friend and colleague Katherine DeFoyd invites me to her Christmas Eve party, and every year I have this sinking feeling. I think I should attend but I never want to. I know I should go because it's meaningful to Katherine and because I really like Katherine, her family, and her friends. I know it would be "good" for me to socialize with them.

Most years, I manage to get myself there... as long as I can arrive early in the evening and leave early. One year I arrived exactly at the appointed hour to find Katherine in the shower and her husband, Gordon, on his way out for ice. I joined him in the search and in subsequent years I became the official bringer-of-the-ice, as they knew I'd get there with it in time!

Arriving early allows me to acclimate myself before others arrive. I can case the situation and find the best spots to hang out. And, most importantly, I can meet people as they come in.

Because I arrive early, people are practically obligated to talk to me because there's no one else for them to talk to! We make eye contact and invariably they walk up and introduce themselves, which is a great relief because I hate introducing myself to strangers and can't bear to seek people out.

If I'm particularly lucky, someone I know also arrives early and I can start a conversation with that person—a conversation I'll try keep alive as long as possible so that I won't have to start one with someone else.

This is what I've done at almost every party or large gathering I've ever attended: find some poor, unsuspecting soul to corner for the entire party. Of course, it's a trifecta if the person in the corner is like me and prefers to have one long chat rather than mingle.

One Christmas, however, I had an earlier commitment and arrived when Katherine's party was in full swing. I was overwhelmed. The party was hopping, and I had to fling myself into the crowd. Everyone was deep in conversation, so I was going to have to approach a group and insinuate myself.

For a while I simply wandered around with a determined look as if I had some destination, when in reality I feared approaching any group and had no destination. I simply thought I wouldn't look as obvious if I stayed in motion as I would if I stood against a wall. It reminded me of bar nights in my 20's.

Interestingly, when I tell this story to fellow introverts, some say they take the opposite approach. My colleague and dear friend Fiona told me she never arrives at a gathering early because she's anxious about not having anyone to talk to and having to stand around by herself, looking obvious. Fiona arrives when a party is in full swing, so she can blend into the crowd and be sure to find someone to talk to.

What to take away from this? For us introverts, large social gatherings are harder to navigate, and good planning helps us manage them successfully. Things are far simpler for extroverts, who as far as I know always say, "Why arrive before the party is hopping?"!

These examples are not meant to send the message to my fellow introverts that they should run for the hills rather than be involved in special events, but rather that they should think these events through and takes steps to make them more manageable.

The first step we introverts should consider is reaching out to a few donors in advance to say we're looking forward to talking to them, as this will give us people to naturally approach at the event.

In fact, this is good fundraising practice in general, and an excellent plan for anyone serving in a cultivation role at your event.

Now let's talk about the event. All is not lost for us introverts! While we might not relish wading into the crowd, and standing around talking might jar our nerves, we're great once we're seated next to someone and can start a one-to-one chat.

For me, personally, the adjacency of someone seated next to me is enough connection to get me more comfortable. In this intimate conversation, I can shine. I can ask lots of questions and truly get to know something about the donor. I can establish a rapport, even with someone I didn't know until that moment. Of course, it will use my energy and I'll still yearn for alone time once the event ends, but I can do my job effectively, and fairly comfortably, in the moment.

Further, especially for our Mission Controllers and our Kindred Spirits whose Secondary Style is Mission Controller, let's not forget that special events take lots of planning and coordination. Special events would implode without attention to timing, flow, coordination, planning, rehearsal, and the like. What are the logistics? How do we manage the flow of traffic? How do we make sure no one takes an extra gift bag? Have you ever met someone who says, "I'm happy keeping the spreadsheet"? That's your Mission Controller, and they're invaluable.

Planning for the largest of our events must start six months or more in advance and stick to a strict calendar. Have the honorees been chosen nine months out? Have we gotten the permit for the 5K from the town five months out?

Now let's talk about the cultivation leading up to, and following up on, our fundraising event. We've talked at length about how valuable introverts are throughout the cultivation process.

That's true for any type of donor, whether major gift, planned gift, institutional, or special event donor. Introverts are great at making those touches throughout the year, whether fueled by the system (Mission Controllers) or by the desire to make others feel good (Kindred Spirits).

All this to say that there are significant roles for introverts before, during, and after events that don't require casual schmoozing or interacting with tons of people. Use us as cultivators. Use us as thankers. Use us as planners. Use us to keep things running smoothly.

And remember—there's a surefire way to tell the difference between introverted and extroverted fundraisers in the context of special events. When your event ends, the extroverts will keep gabbing until the lights are shut off, and then propose to whoever's left that they go somewhere to debrief or continue the party. That's because the extroverts have derived their energy from others and are totally revved up. We introverts, assuming we managed to stay to the end (as fundraisers we generally have to), decline all such invitations and head home to have quiet time by ourselves. Do you stay or run?!

Chapter Eleven

Introverts and Other Fundraising Roles

Introverts bring strengths to every aspect of fundraising, which is key as so many of us are in small shops where we wear every hat. Whether we're playing multiple roles or specializing in just one piece of the fundraising puzzle, we have much to offer.

Planned Giving

I've always seen planned gifts as an important subset of major gifts, and they're a great match for an introvert's skill set.

Of course, many planned gifts come as a surprise and weren't based on a proactive relationship on the part of the organization. By proactive, I mean an instance where we identified a donor who we thought could also be a planned gift donor, and we reached out to have planned giving conversations that led to them making a planned gift.

Here we're talking about the planned gifts we proactively cultivate and solicit. And here, introverts shine.

If there were ever a donor relationship based on listening, it's the relationship with a planned gift prospect. It's a relationship based on coming to understand what our donor wants to accomplish over the long term; what they'd like their legacy to be. And it's often a conversation the donor has never had before, so treading lightly and listening for clues is paramount.

What do they hope to accomplish after they depart this world? Are they trying to make sure they continue to have an impact? Are they wanting to secure the fiscal health of a cause they love? Are they trying to set an example for their children? Do they want to make a gift that benefits them financially now so that their retirement is secured?

These are questions that speak to a donor's life story and, in so many ways, introverts are perfectly positioned to ask them. In addition to listening more and talking less, which allows them to learn more, our Kindred Spirits and Mission Controllers have other key skills to use in planned giving conversations.

Kindred Spirits will bond by sharing their own legacy thoughts and showing great empathy for whatever concerns the donors have about their future plans. And they'll be sensitive to the delicate nature of many of these donor discussions.

Mission Controllers will understand that planned gifts require a process on the part of the donor. The process starts with thinking —often for the first time—about this idea of legacy, and continues with the figuring out how to make one's desires a reality. The donor might not have a will yet or might need to revise their will. This can all take a good deal of time, which plays to the Mission Controller's patience.

I asked my friend and planned giving expert Tony Martignetti, of Martignetti Planned Giving Advisors and Planned Giving Accelerator, for his thoughts on introverts and planned giving:

> "I'm a Go-Getter/Kindred Spirit and I heavily rely on my Kindred Spirit side in planned giving.
>
> I think intuitive folks are active, engaged listeners. Not just hearing but actively listening to what people are saying. And putting some effort into remembering what people are saying. Which might mean taking notes.
>
> Most of the people I talk to are over 70 or 80. I'm 60. They have rich stories about being children in the Great Depression, being in World War II, being Vietnam veterans. My Kindred Spirit wants to absorb these stories and listen, and the more you listen to folks and are curious about people— asking follow-up questions—the more they'll be drawn to you. People give to organizations with people they like.
>
> My experience, in planned giving, is you eventually get to the point when you've been attentive and caring and have built the relationship to where they come forward and say they're ready to make a gift—or another gift.
>
> We need to keep in mind planned gifts are on the donor's timetable. The donor might agree to put your organization in their will, but they won't physically do that until they

write or revise their will. The timetable is different, and it takes someone who's good at saying to themselves, "We've got to slow down the process to be on the donor's timetable." This plays to the introvert's strengths.

It's a selflessness of subjugating your needs to the needs of the donor, and I think that's something introverts, especially Kindred Spirits, do best."

To close our thoughts on planned giving, there's another strength our analytic introverts (Mission Controllers) have. While most planned gifts are simple bequests in wills, many of the most significant planned gifts are in fact gift annuities, charitable remainder trusts, the bequeathing of land and other assets, and more. Here's where Mission Controllers shine. Their strength in planning and implementing systems will help them learn about and appreciate these technical planned gifts. They'll have the ability to describe them accurately to donors, and to take care of all the paperwork and process on the organization's side.

Institutional Fundraising

Introverts make great institutional fundraisers...especially our Mission Controllers. Without doubt they excel at research and writing, both key elements. They're planful, which is key to the work as it is process-driven. Think of the planning side of special events, as many of the same skills apply here: developing and sticking to calendars, paying attention to details, developing written materials, etc.

But we all know institutional fundraising—even much government funding—is based on relationships. Here the relationships are not with the donors themselves, but with the grants officers and elected officials who make the decisions. All the great skills introverts bring to their relationships with individual donors they bring to these relationships as well.

Direct Mail, Annual Appeals, And Research

All I'll say here is...Go Mission Controllers! What would we do without your amazing attention to detail, to systems, to the step-by-step execution of detailed plans? So many parts of fundraising, such as these, require someone willing to dive deep and stay focused. Someone who will do the quiet, detailed work that is critically important but can remain unseen. Someone who is happy to work solo. Just as we've discussed in terms of special events, organization and an aptitude for process are key.

Further, the written word requires the same focus on building relationships as the one-to-one conversation. Direct mail and annual appeals rely on the ability of the author to tell a compelling story. In fact, have you ever wondered why a general solicitation letter is often long? It's because it's written to tons of donors at once, all of whom find different things compelling. Therefore, the letter must appeal to these various people by focusing on goals (Rainmaker donors), vision/opportunity (Go-Getter donors), heart (Kindred Spirits) and plan (Mission Controllers). That means there's a role for introverts in helping craft the wording of general fundraising letters to assure they appeal to a wide range of donors.

Chapter Twelve

Introverts Make
Excellent Fundraising
Board Members

For small and mid-sized organizations, our board members are key to our fundraising efforts. Ninety percent of all nonprofits have budgets under $1 million, and that means they can only afford to have one or two development staff, if any at all. These organizations don't have major gifts officers whose time is fully dedicated to cultivating and soliciting individual gifts. And they certainly don't operate like universities and hospitals, which today can have dozens of gift officers. We need our board members to help us fundraise, as our executive directors, and development staff, if any, can only do so much.

In small to mid-sized organizations, much of that board fundraising has historically been through special events and letter appeals. Those efforts raise significant dollars, but the gifts are often one-offs due to a board member leaning on their relationships in one way or another. To be sure, those are helpful gifts in the short run, but their transactional nature means that they come and go. I think board members can play a greater fundraising role.

Our boards, if properly developed, can serve in lieu of major gifts staff, and greatly expand the amount of this work that can get done. I like to think of my board members as mini major-gifts officers, each with a small portfolio (my magic number is four) of individual relationships they cultivate and steward over time. Imagine if everyone on your board helped, particularly in the ongoing cultivation, education, involvement, and personalized thanking of donors. If each board member gave two hours a month to major gifts work. Combined, you would accomplish a tremendous amount of major gifts work each year.

Everything we've said about fundraisers in this book also applies to board members and the major gift work they do. Each board member has their own Asking Style, and therefore each board member is going to have different strengths and challenges as they go out to help with this work.

Our Kindred Spirit board members are going to be the most empathic and will be most caring and attentive to our donors. They're the ones most likely to reach out just to see how the donors they're cultivating are doing, or naturally think to send the donors an update that seems relevant.

Mission Controllers are the board members we can most rely on to do their work. Give them a set of tasks and they'll come up with a plan or system for completing those tasks. They'll do their homework, and they'll keep everyone well-informed on their progress.

To support introverted fundraising board members in their work, it's important to realize a few things.

First, when training your board, keep in mind that introverts might struggle in group settings, so be sure to break people out into small groups where introverts will feel more comfortable. Also, consider one-to-one training/coaching for introverted board members. They're more likely to ask questions and express their concerns individually.

Next, keep in mind that everyone will develop their own personal story to share with donors. This means respecting a Kindred Spirit's desire to tell a heart story and a Mission Controller's desire to tell a plan story. Even in a very data-driven organization (e.g., a former client, The Environmental Defense Fund), heart and plan stories can be equally effective.

When Kindred Spirits bring the heart, sharing deeply personal stories of why they care enough to be board members, this deep emotion will be palpable to donors. When Mission Controller board members share the organization's plans in detail, it shows they're deeply involved and understand what the organization is doing. This makes a great impression on donors, who will feel comfort in knowing the board is involved at this level.

Next, match donor communication to your board member's Style. Encouraging introverted board members to communicate with donors by email and text will give them permission to be themselves. If your instructions are to reach out to call no matter what, your introverts could chafe at that and put off their tasks. Let's not forget, as we've said before, that half our donors are also introverts and prefer written communication, so there's no rationale for asking your board members to call everyone anyway.

Finally, the rules of partnering are key here. Kindred Spirit and Mission Controller board members are particularly good partners for Rainmakers and Go-Getters (either staff or fellow board members), especially if your donors are more introverted.

Boards and Fundraising Events

Though we've talked about events already, it's important to touch on them through the lens of board fundraising. Putting aside my belief that much of event-based board fundraising is nonstrategic and soul-deadening, the burden on introverted fundraisers vis a vis fundraising events is problematic. I see organizations continuously strong-arm or guilt introverted board members into fundraising for, and attending, these events. At many organizations, it's a requirement baked into the board member job description. Why?

Putting such an emphasis on large fundraising events is at best putting our introverted board members in a difficult, uncomfortable position. At worst, it may be keeping important voices and leaders from even joining those boards.

I'm a firm believer that every board member should fundraise to the best of their ability, but asking everyone to put their efforts into large fundraising events is no different than asking everyone to be on the finance committee whether it's an area of interest and expertise...or not.

Why not marshal introverted board members where they can shine—in building individual relationships? Bring them along on visits to funders to show strong board involvement and leadership. Introduce them to major individual donors so they can form meaningful relationships that strengthen the donors' ties to the organization. Have them serve as ambassadors at small cultivation events where they can pair off with prospective donors to have rich conversations.

Strong, Diverse Boards Lead to Strong Board Fundraising

The key to board fundraising is for everyone to do it. And if we want everyone to buy into the concept of fundraising, not only must we help board members do the fundraising that plays to their strengths, but we must make certain the board is cohesive and collegial. It needs to be well-run and focused on long-term strategic goals, with respect for all and a sense of camaraderie. And it needs to represent a diverse set of opinions.

Over the years I've worked with more than 100 boards, and since the development of the Asking Styles, I've analyzed boards through this lens. Hands down, the strongest boards have had a mix of Asking Styles, and those boards were the most consistently involved in fundraising. Here's why.

As we know, each Style brings a range of strengths and challenges to the table...a different perspective and voice:

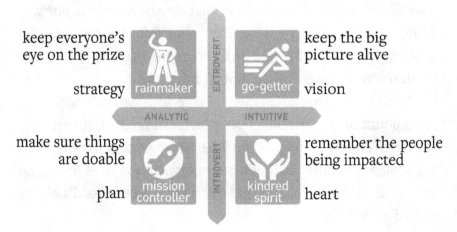

keep everyone's eye on the prize		keep the big picture alive
strategy — rainmaker	EXTROVERT	go-getter — vision
	ANALYTIC · INTUITIVE	
make sure things are doable		remember the people being impacted
plan — mission controller	INTROVERT	kindred spirit — heart

While extroverts tend to look to the future boldly, they can sometimes miss important parts of the puzzle introverts are more attuned to.

Rainmakers are great at setting goals and working hard to attain them. However, in the execution, they sometimes get so caught up in outcomes and performance measurements that they can lose sight of the fact that the efforts that improve lives aren't always the most efficient efforts. Kindred Spirits are key to making sure we don't forget that, at the end of the day, we're talking about people. We're not making widgets; we're impacting people's lives. Sometimes the most economical solution is not the best one.

We love Go-Getters for their passion and enthusiasm for going big. The biggest ideas, the ones that help us see the world and its solutions differently, often come from Go-Getters. However, sometimes Go-Getters need a reality check. Someone needs to make sure their ideas are doable. Enter Mission controllers, who immediately grasp what it would take to turn ideas into action.

Now imagine any discussion or planning process that doesn't have all four voices at the table. It's liable to be skewed in one way or another. If it's skewed, it's probably not going to be as strategic or strong as it could be. And if the board isn't strong in its work, it's doubtful it will be strong in its fundraising.

Given the fact that board membership automatically requires a fair amount of group interaction, which can favor extroverts and tax introverts, it's imperative to be aware of this dynamic and work hard to counter it. If not, your organization risks having no introverts at the table, and this will weaken your board's ability to lead effectively.

The Voice of Introverts
At Board Meetings

Let's assume we've got a good range of Styles at the table. Given the introvert/extrovert dichotomy in particular, the challenge then comes in giving us introverts the opportunity to share our opinions.

Imagine your last board meeting. Who spoke up? Who was silent?

As we now know, introverts are far less likely to chime in during large group discussions. This is particularly true if people are asked to chime in voluntarily. If the chair asks whether anyone has any comments, the extroverts will speak up first since they talk to think, while the introverts will still be formulating their questions. Mission Controllers will take the longest to respond, before doing so thoughtfully and fully. Kindred Spirits will not want to interrupt, and if they're shy it will be even harder for them to jump in. You can begin to see how, especially if there's only so much time for discussion, the introverts' thoughts might not be shared.

Yet all things being equal, the ideas of introverts are just as important as those of extroverts, so how do you make sure introverted board members are heard? How do you make sure their ideas are validated so that they feel part of the team?

It's up to the board chair or discussion leader to ensure everyone's voice is heard. Perhaps they go around the table to make sure everyone has a chance to speak. Or they call on those who have been silent? Or they find out in advance of a meeting who would like to speak during it. Perhaps they even gather all the input and feedback in advance and present the findings to date so introverts can see that their ideas have been validated.

This has become even more critical in the age of virtual meetings. I'm sure you have experienced the challenge of multiple people trying to speak up at once in a Zoom room. Online it's harder to read the cues, harder to tell when someone else is trying to speak. This can effectively silence introverts.

Yet have you noticed how, often after everyone has spoken, someone who's been quiet adds their voice and it's something revelational? That would be your introvert speaking. So, making sure all board member voices are heard is key to strong decisions.

To come full circle, making sure introverted board members' voices are heard not only leads to a stronger board, but to those introverted board members feeling more integral to the workings of the organization. To the extent they feel a deeper connection to our organization due to their input being heard and taken seriously, they will be more inclined to do the hardest work, the fundraising, on its behalf.

Chapter Thirteen

What Does This Mean For You Extroverts?

As highlighted by me and by others throughout this book, there is a natural tendency—in fundraising, as in society at large—to devalue introverts. A natural tendency to extol those who are the life of the party, and to scorn others as "party poopers." To somehow think that enjoying big social events has some higher status than enjoying quiet times. Or that leadership requires extroversion.

In *The Extrovert's Guide to Elevating Introverted Leaders in the Workplace*, David Boroughs shares that "In corporate America, headwinds...make it unnecessarily harder for one group to succeed...the headwinds blow much stronger on the introverted side. Common headwinds, like the prevalence of similarity bias in many corporate performance evaluations and selection processes, make it much more difficult for the introverted aspiring leader to succeed, even to just be seen."[7]

The numbers underscore this. Boroughs points to a 2009 study in *Industrial and Organizational Psychology* that found "those with below average levels of extroversion...make up only 12% of supervisors, 7% of first-line managers, 5% of mid-level managers, 3% of executives, and 2% of top executives."[8]

And while we can hope the last 14 years have brought some enlightenment and the numbers are improving, we can be sure they nowhere reflect the capacity of introverts to lead. For successful leadership is not based on extroversion. It's based on intelligence, acumen, good listening skills, high executive function, strategic thinking, collegiality, and other key traits.

In this context, let's talk about board leadership a bit more, as most of you reading this book are involved in smaller nonprofits where the board chair's ability to lead the board to fundraise is paramount to the organization's success.

My dear departed colleague and friend, Michael Davidson, taught me much before he passed away in 2022. Michael was a rower and loved rowing analogies. He likened boards to rowing teams, which are only as good as their weakest rower. The strongest team is one where everyone is strong together and in sync with each other, and that only happens with a strong coxswain.

---

7   Boroughs, David. The Extrovert's Guide to Elevating Introverted Leaders in the Workplace. Introverts and Belonging LLC, 2022.

8   Boroughs, 2022

Boards might be even more reliant on good leadership and teamwork than other group structures. Here you've got a bunch of volunteers willingly giving of their time, talent, and treasure. And they're much more likely to give more of all three when they feel they are respected, heard, and valued, and feel good about their work.

That only happens with good leadership, and good leadership is hard to find. We've got more than 1.5 million nonprofits in the United States alone, and each one needs a good leader. That is hard to achieve, and even harder if introverts are going to be devalued because they don't fit the stereotype of a leader. When extroverts devalue us, they risk putting in place leadership inferior to what an introverted leader might bring.

The fallout from this goes far beyond leadership issues and positions. Devaluation by extroverts can lead us introverts to devalue ourselves, as we see the extroverts get rewarded more often. When we're passed over for positions because we're too quiet or we don't thrive at the company picnic, we can feel we've done something wrong. That we're not up to the task. That we're missing the secret sauce to lead. We can look at social butterflies and wish we could be like that—believing that if we just worked the crowd, we could rise through the management ranks.

Yet extroverts ignore us at their peril. Putting my obvious bias out there...you extroverts need us a lot if our organizations are going to succeed.

You need us to partner with you to best serve your donors and build the strongest relationships.

You need us to do the listening while you're talking...and politely intercede when you're talking too much.

You need us because your introverted donors might feel a certain comfort with other introverts, and that might allow them to build closer ties with your organization.

You Rainmakers need to partner with Kindred Spirits to make sure that your donors are front and center, we're catering to their needs, and they feel heard and appreciated.

You Go-Getters need to partner with Mission Controllers to make sure there's a plan and it's followed, to keep meetings on track, and to dot the i's and cross the t's.

Ninette Enrique, Chief Advancement Officer for The Hotch-kiss School (Rainmaker/Mission Controller), had this to share:

> "As an extrovert and Rainmaker, I love going to events, working the room, and chatting with everyone. I would not ask the introverted fundraisers on my team to do this, and I don't think it hampers their ability to be great fundraisers.
>
> If an introverted fundraiser does not feel comfortable speaking with multiple people at an event, they can hone in on one or two donor prospects. At a recent event, a fundraiser on my team focused on one donor the entire evening and really moved that relationship along. As a result, Hotchkiss received a seven-figure gift.
>
> Introverted fundraisers shine when they meet with donors individually. They excel at building deep, personal connections. For solicitations, I think sending two solicitors to a meeting is best. Ideally one is an extrovert and the other is an introvert, so they balance each other and also reflect the donor with whom they are meeting."

Extroverts—we admire you greatly for all the qualities you embody. We often wish we had those qualities. Yet we don't ask you to wish you had our qualities—only to admire us for them.

Chapter Fourteen

Introverts Rock!

It's so easy to assume one way is the right way. Or to assume everyone will respond similarly to the same gesture or opportunity. But doing so puts us at a great disadvantage in fundraising, as elsewhere.

If we introverted fundraisers believe we have to be something or other in order to be successful, we risk devaluing ourselves or not being authentic in how we act. If we're managing introverted fundraisers or board members, we risk not taking advantage of all the incredible skills they bring to the table. If we assume all our donors are extroverted, and focus too heavily on special events, we won't reach half our donors in a way that makes them feel heard and appreciated.

Here's my most amusing, and maybe most telling, story. I saved it for last.

Personal Story III

In 2019, I was asked to be a major presenter at the Harold Grinspoon Foundation's Life & Legacy Program Conference. Not only that, but the Foundation had bought copies of my book for every attendee. I was a main attraction.

The conference opened with a reception the first night, and the prospect of it had loomed over me for days. Now, up in my hotel room, I started texting my friend, Joyce, saying how much I dreaded the thought of heading down to the reception—a sea of people where I knew exactly two of them: my Foundation contact and a fellow presenter. Two out of 200...and that was if the other presenter had gotten there in time for the reception (nope!).

Down at the reception I started my usual dance of moving around the room as if I had some destination - heading out to the hallway and back multiple times, getting some food, and generally keeping in motion until I eventually ended up in my favorite spot—against a wall.

There was a group of guests chatting close by, and a gentleman in the group noticed I was standing there by myself. Soon enough, and to my horror, he approached me. Being gracious, he said, "I see you're standing here by yourself—why don't you come join our group." I cringed as this meant meeting a whole group of people at the same time, but I had been hired for the gig and couldn't turn him down.

Well, as I entered the group, a lady turned to me and said, "Wait, aren't you the guy on the back of the book?!"

I was mortified and blushed. Here I was, a main attraction, and I had been standing against the wall, wishing not to mingle with those who had come to the conference to learn from me.

Well, I'll always wish I had what it takes to dive into a crowd of strangers. I know that all things being equal, it would have been great for my career, and probably good for my ego too! But I can take comfort in knowing that my ability to build meaningful relationships one-to-one has led to an extraordinary fundraising career filled with numerous successes.

I'm sure that if I'd joined conference participants at the bar, they would have told me they loved my presentation, and that would have made my day. I'm sure that if I'd worked the room at Hudson Guild's community dinner, I could have developed a new potential major donor. I'm sure that if I mingled more at Katherine's parties, I could have made some good, new friends. But in my own way I developed countless major donors, and I've got a great set of close friends I made over the years, one at a time.

I'm sure having more comfort on the phone would have been helpful, but I know I wrote wonderful, personal emails during the past 30 years that helped deepen scores of donor relationships.

Now I know it was totally okay to be me and that I should have been proud of what I did all those years, rather than knock myself about what I didn't do.

Boy, I wish I knew then what I know now. I wish I could have shared all this with all the extraordinary fundraisers, executive directors, and board members who I saw question their skills over the years.

At least I can now share what I've learned. That no one has it all. No one. And that we rock.

I am a great fundraiser, and so are my fellow introverts. We just have a different playbook. We play to our strengths and work to compensate for our challenges just as extroverts do. And while the world often sees extroversion as strength, I hope this book has helped my fellow fundraisers—both introverts and extroverts—see introverts for all they have to offer. Go introverts!

Discussion Questions

1. What are the top five things I will take away from this book to apply to my life and my work? How might I conduct myself differently given what I've learned? How might I value myself and others more?

2. Who are the three donors I interact with most often? Where on the introvert/extrovert spectrum do I think they are? How does that impact my interactions with them? What might I do differently to cater to this difference? Is there someone I might partner with to deepen the relationship between these donors and my organization?

3. How much of our organization's donor cultivation is done through large events and how much is done through small cultivation events and individual meetings? Are we making sure our introverted donors get as much strategic cultivation as our extroverted donors?

4. What was the last fundraising event our organization produced? Who are the five donors we hoped to have there who declined? Taking a stab at where they are on the introvert/extrovert spectrum, might any of them have declined due to being introverts? If so, might we have approached them differently? Could we have made them comfortable enough to attend? Or what other types of events or gatherings might draw them in instead?

5. What was the last large work event I attended, and how did I navigate it? Are there things I might do differently going forward, through the introvert/extrovert lens, to honor my, and everyone's, comfort level and areas of expertise?

6. Who is my most frequent cultivation and solicitation partner? How do I see our dynamic in meetings with donors through the introverted/extroverted spectrum, and how might I better plan future meetings given what I know now?

7. Where on the introverted/extroverted spectrum is my boss, and how does that impact our dynamic? Is this something I can point out to them as a means for improving our working relationship?

8. Where on the introverted/extroverted spectrum are my direct reports, and how does that impact how I need to manage and support them?

9. What are the Asking Styles of everyone on our team (staff or board), and how does this impact how we work together? Can we better understand the dynamic of our meetings through this lens? Are there adjustments we might make to better suit the introverts (and, by extension, everyone) on our team?

10. Who are the three people I am closest to in the world? Are they on the introverted or extroverted side of the spectrum, and can I see how this shapes each of those relationships?

Exercise 1: Partnering in a Meeting

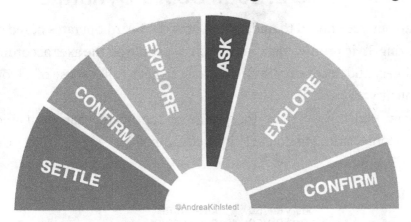

- Break up into groups of three where, ideally, at least one person is a Kindred Spirit or Mission Controller. Two will play askers and one will play a donor.

- If there's only one introvert, that person should be one of the two fundraisers.

- If you have a group of four, have two donors.

- Walk through the Arc of the Ask and discuss how to have an intentional conversation:

    - How might your Styles impact how the meeting unfolds?

    - What roles might be better suited to one or the other of you?

    - What do you have to watch out for given your Styles? And the Style of the donor?

- Come back together and discuss what people learned about themselves (at least three or four examples)

Exercise 2: Your Board Dynamic

Map out your board to understand how the board operates based on its Asking Style profile. Make sure to place people on the axes according to Primary and Secondary Styles, so you can get a fuller sense of all four personality traits.

Below, you can see how the profile of the board changes if Alice and George are Mission Controller/Rainmakers rather than Go-Getter/Rainmakers:

Once everyone is mapped out, have your board discuss the following:

- What about the mapping surprises us…or not?
- Can we see where our board's profile has impacted how our organization makes decisions?
- Is there a Style that's particularly under-represented, and might we recruit people of that Style? What would we hope they'd bring to the table?
- How might our board's profile impact how we are involved in fundraising?
- Can we see how various board members might partner to complement each other based on Style?

Exercise 3: Find Your Words And Tell Your Story

The goal is to tell a passionate story that is authentic to who each person is. The story should try to focus on the organization's vision and the impact it is trying to make.

- Break up into groups of three. If one or two are left, add each to a group of three.

- In each group:

  - Ask each person to answer one of these questions in 60 seconds:

    - Why do you love your organization?

    - Tell me about your organization?

    - What is the goal of your organization?

  - Someone should keep time and each story must stop at 60 seconds.

  - After everyone has told their story, discuss the following:

    - What was compelling about my/your story?

    - Can we see where our Asking Styles impacted how we told our story?

    - Did we discuss vision and impact?

  - If time allows, have everyone tell their story one more time.

- Bring the groups back together and have one person from each group report on their experience.

About the Author

Brian Saber is one of the field's preeminent experts on the art and science of asking for charitable gifts face-to-face, and he has been working with nonprofit organizations for more than 35 years to help unlock their fundraising potential. Brian has personally solicited thousands of donors as a director of development, executive director, board member/chair, and consultant.

Brian harnessed all that frontline experience to become a sought-after trainer, coach, and consultant across the U.S. and abroad. His work is transformative. He leads workshops and trainings, presents webinars, delivers keynotes, and coaches top-level staff and board members, taking organizations to the next level.

In 2008, Brian co-founded Asking Matters, the most comprehensive online resource on asking in the field. Asking Matters is home to the Asking Styles, a revolutionary concept in the field that helps people understand and embrace their unique strengths as fundraisers. Asking Matters offers courses, webinars, and other virtual and in-person training opportunities. It also hosts the popular Fundraising Masters series.

Brian has led training programs and presented at conferences for the Arthritis Foundation, Prevent Child Abuse America, the Archdiocese of Los Angeles, the Environmental Defense Fund, Social Venture Partners International, National Public Radio, Volunteers of America, the U.S. Olympic Committee, The Salvation Army, Boys and Girls Clubs of America, AFP International, numerous AFP chapters, the North American YMCA Development Conference, and others.

Brian is the author of three other books: *Asking Styles: Revolutionize Your Fundraising*, hailed by the late Jerry Panas as "the best antidote I've read on taking the fear out of asking," *Boards and Asking Styles: A Roadmap to Success*, and *Engaged Boards Will Fundraise: How Good Governance Inspires Them*.

Acknowledgments

I must start by thanking Susan Cain and so many other people who have studied introverts and pleaded their case. Their work has opened my eyes to who I am and why I act as I do, and it has given me extraordinary insight into the dynamics of introverts in fundraising.

Thank you as well to everyone who contributed content directly to this book: Ninette Enrique, Debbie Hammer, Andrea Kihlstedt, Esther Landau, Tony Martignetti, and Steve Taylor. Your experiences and your willingness to share them have been so important.

I owe so much to my team. I am forever in debt to Aliyah Baruchin, my editor. This book, in particular, was quite challenging to write, and her insightful feedback every step of the way made this into the book it is. I owe so much to Thomas Edward West, my publisher and designer, whose talents are endless. Huge thanks to my book marketing guru, Robin Blakely. Along with Aliyah and Tom, she has incredible wisdom and has been instrumental in giving this book the launch it deserves.

Always a thanks to the rest of my team: Kyle Nunes, who keeps Asking Matters going every day, Shannon Welch, Michele Ericson-Stern, Jodi Chromey, and Gary Ziffer. I'm lucky to have you along on this ride with me.

There would be no Asking Matters and no Asking Styles without Andrea Kihlstedt. Endless thanks to my dear friend, my colleague, and my former business partner, as it was her original idea that blossomed into the Styles.

I must acknowledge my friend and collaborator, Michael Davidson, whom we lost in 2022. Over the 20 years we knew each other, he taught me just about everything I know about boards.

Many thanks to all my bosses who, over the years, just let me run with it. I was never very good at being managed (probably too sensitive to take productive feedback) and their trust in me allowed me to do what I do best—form relationships with donors. A special shout-out to Ron Manderschied, Nancy Winship, and Janice McGuire.

A huge thanks to all my fellow fundraisers. Our work isn't easy, and generally it isn't fun, but it's critically important and I appreciate you for doing the work that raises the funds to allow the nonprofit world to impact countless lives.

I am grateful to all my clients. I am very lucky to have spent my entire career in the nonprofit world, and the last 15 years as a consultant have been incredibly rewarding. Every day I get to learn about the extraordinary, important work you all are doing to make the world a better place.

Last, but never least, I thank my son, Richard. He is my world.

About Asking Matters™

Brian Saber & Andrea Kihlstedt, two experienced fundraising professionals, believed when it came to raising money, the primary limiting factor was people's reluctance to ask for gifts. Andrea, a capital campaign consultant, and Brian, a front-line fundraiser and consultant, decided to develop a set of practical, accessible tools to help staff and board members learn the art and science of asking and find the courage and will to ask.

Through her work on capital campaigns, Andrea knew that when the stakes were high enough to get people to ask, the results were remarkable, with organizations often raising far more money than anyone thought possible. And Brian, a front-line fundraiser who has asked thousands of people for hundreds of millions of dollars of gifts, knew it was possible to overcome one's fears and ask...and ask and ask. He believed that, while it might never get easy and often isn't fun, the results were well worth the discomfort and often yielded much more than money.

In 2009, Brian and Andrea launched Asking Matters, a company that uses web-based learning and in-person training to provide the information and inspiration needed to motivate staff and board members to ask. In 2013 Brian acquired Andrea's share, and he continues to own and run the company today.

Index

Also by Brian Saber

ISBN: 978-1720610281
Paperback: $24.95
eBook: $19.95

THE BREAKTHROUGH CONCEPT OF THE ASKING STYLES makes it possible for anyone to become a more effective fundraiser. Your Asking Style is based on your personality and unique set of strengths when asking for gifts.

If you've ever said to yourself "I'm not a fundraiser" or "I don't fit the stereotype," embracing your Asking Style will change your entire mindset. Once you understand your strengths—and challenges—you'll be comfortable, confident and effective. You'll have a roadmap for dealing with donors. You'll know what to say, how to conduct meetings, and how to close gifts.

ISBN: 978-1733087520
Paperback: $19.95
eBook: $14.95

A STRONGER BOARD LEADS TO GREATER IMPACT! Your organization cannot achieve its vision without a strong board. A strong board starts with bringing on the right people, but then it's about working together effectively, understanding leadership and board dynamics, supporting board members appropriately so you can do your best work, having you fundraise in a way that suits who you are, and more.

In his second book, Brian Saber uses the Asking Styles lens to help you build your board's strength. He'll help you understand how you and your fellow board members operate individually and collectively, what strengths you bring to the table, and how to employ those to best advantage.

By Michael Davidson and Brian Saber

ISBN: 979-8469760801
Paperback: $19.95
eBook: $14.95

FUNDRAISING IS THE HARDEST WORK YOU ASK YOUR BOARD MEMBERS TO DO. If they're not fully committed and engaged and they don't feel they have a strong stake in your organization, they aren't going to fundraise for it.

In this groundbreaking book, Michael Davidson and Brian Saber bring their collective expertise and their 20 years of working together on governance and fundraising issues to help you understand how good governance is a means to inspire your board to fundraise.